DINNER CHURCH

DINNER CHURCH

*Building Bridges
by Breaking Bread*

Verlon Fosner

 Seedbed

Scripture quotations are taken from the Holy Bible, New Living Translation, copyright 1996, 2004. Used by permission of Tyndale House Publishers, Inc., Wheaton, Illinois 60189. All rights reserved.

Scripture quotations marked esv are taken from The Holy Bible, English Standard Version. ESV® Permanent Text Edition® (2016). Copyright © 2001 by Crossway Bibles, a publishing ministry of Good News Publishers.

Scripture quotations marked KJV are taken from the Holy Bible, King James Version, Cambridge, 1796.

Printed in the United States of America

Cover design by Strange Last Name
Page design by PerfecType

Fosner, Verlon.
  Dinner, church : building bridges by breaking bread / Verlon Fosner. – Frankin, Tennessee : Seedbed Publishing, ©2017.

       183 ; 21 cm.

       ISBN 9781628243888 (paperback : alk. paper)
       ISBN 9781628243895 (Mobi)
       ISBN 9781628243901 (ePub)
       ISBN 9781628243918 (uPDF)

       1. Evangelistic work--United States. 2. Dinners and dining--Religious aspects--Christianity. 3. Hospitality--Religious aspects--Christianity. 4. Church development, New--United States. 5. Westminster Community Church (Shoreline, Wash.)
       I. Title.

BV3790 .F677 2017   269/.2   2017934498

SEEDBED PUBLISHING
Franklin, Tennessee
Seedbed.com

This book is dedicated to my wife, Melodee. Her indomitable spirit during the dark days of failure breathed life into me. And her tireless work in setting tables for the left-behind was a constant inspiration. She is my Jonathan.

CONTENTS

INTRODUCTION

Christianity is the greatest rescue project the world has ever seen. If the scriptural phrase "the day of salvation" means anything, it means that we are living in a special season—the season of rescue. And yet, we found that our church in Seattle was shrinking. Somehow we had become completely ineffective at rescuing the lost. To add insult to injury, we were located in the fastest-growing city in America. Certainly you would think that somebody, anybody, who wanted to go to heaven with us would move to town. But no, we just continued to decline year after year.

However, God did not forget about us. Through a series of interventions that can only be explained as divine downloads, we got a glimpse of doing church in a different way. And if the miracle of a fresh vision was not enough, our then eighty-five-year-old church found our second wind. A lionlike boldness roared out of our souls, and we walked off of our church campus to do church in Seattle neighborhoods. We had a strange form of church in our hands, but we had a sense of calling in our hearts.

Within weeks of planting our first dinner church in a community space sixty blocks south of our campus, we realized we were witnessing a divine spark. What was happening during those evenings was unexplainable.

The room started filling up with strangers, sinners, seculars, and broken people. And for the first time in our lives, healing flowed naturally and evangelism was easy.

Since those first days in 2007, we have spent a great deal of time trying to define what was happening in our rooms night after night. What follows is not only our rebirth story, but also my paltry efforts to describe the divine spark that has been showing up in our dinner churches. While we continue to see depths of the dinner table theology unfold before us, these are our clearest observations and interpretations to date.

1

THE DAY WE REALIZED
WE HAD CANCER

*"A man planted a fig tree in his garden and
came again and again to see if there was any
fruit on it, but he was always disappointed. . . .
The gardener answered, 'Sir, give it one more
chance. . . . I'll give it special attention and
plenty of fertilizer. If we get figs next year,
fine. If not, then you can cut it down.'"*
—Luke 13:6, 8–9

An awkward silence filled the room, and a sick feeling
formed in the pit of our stomachs. It was 2004, and thirty
core leaders had agreed to meet on Tuesday nights to
talk about the future of our church. Our historic group,
Westminster Community Church, had done very well
in Seattle since 1923. Our natural charm, good-looking
people, and ample money had kept us thriving for
many decades, or at least we thought we were thriving.
However, the past three years had been a different story.
For no visible reason, we started to decline by 14 percent
per year in both attendance and finances. These declines
prompted our Tuesday-night leadership meetings.

We talked about church models, urbanization, and evangelism, until one particular night. No one in the room saw this coming, including me. I remember asking an innocent question: "How would the neighbors know Jesus if he lived at our church address?" The group merged images of Jesus from Scripture with the life of our North Seattle community and collectively envisioned a Jesus who would walk into the lives of our neighbors with friendship, laughter, healing, and favor.

That first question inspired a second question: "Well, how do our neighbors know us?" And that was where the wheels came off the bus; that was the awkward-silence moment. Everyone in the room knew the answer, but no one wanted to admit it. Finally, a brave soul blurted out with a frustrated chuckle, "They don't know us. All we ever do is come in and out of this building." Then there was more awkward silence as the leaders looked around the room at one another, and some just looked at the floor. That was the exact moment in the life of our church when we knew there was something terribly wrong with our version of Christianity. We were a group of Christ-followers who did not look like our Master. We had cancer; something had eaten away our Christian vitality and we had turned into something different from an expression of Christ. We were sick!

Consumer Christians

Looking back, it is obvious that cancer had been forming in us for years. The idea of having a church full of saved people who only came on Sundays and left a few dollars in the offering plate had not served us well. With such a shallow mission as increasing our attendance, well-meaning Christians started to think like congregants with political power and alliances, each lobbying for dollars to be steered toward his or her favorite program—consumer Christians. Business meetings had been battlefields; places where rancor and head shaking were normal.

One business meeting turned into an attempt to prove that I, as the pastor, had embezzled $97,000 from church funds and used it to remodel my house. That turned into a six-month investigation of audits, network officials, and long board meetings. While at the end I was exonerated because no money was missing, the incident took a certain toll on our lives, particularly my wife, Melodee.

Ironically, "staff" infection gave me staph infection. In other words, some of the church staff who had been critical of me behind my back created so much stress in my body that I actually broke out with a rare form of *Staphylococcus* that took weeks and series of shots to reverse. After all, if the embezzlement charges were proven, I wasn't just leaving town—I was going to jail. These were stressful days.

However, my struggles were minor-league compared to what the experience did to my wife. It was painful beyond words when large portions of our congregation stopped talking to us, suspecting that the charges were true. People we had eaten with were now avoiding us in the halls of the church. At one point, Melodee stopped playing the piano and ceased coming to Sunday gatherings for a few months to stay home and heal. It still amazes us how few people reached out to ask her where she was and how she was doing. One lady thought the appropriate form of care for Melodee was a note rebuking her for not taking her place in the front row to encourage the people.

One of the hallmarks of churches with consumer Christians is the rate of burnout among their pastors. Brooklyn Tabernacle pastor and author Jim Cymbala reported that American pastors are now leaving the ministry at the rate of fifty per day.[1] I am sure that some of these resignations are the natural ebb and flow of life, but this exaggerated and growing number is evidence of the pressures brought on by the consumer cancer that is festering in many American churches. We had it too, and the leaders sitting around the circle that fateful night knew it.

Behavioral Christlikeness

What do you do when you find out your church has cancer? Answering that question became our leadership challenge. The week before had proven beyond all doubt that our version of Christianity did not look like the life of Christ, so all I knew to do at the next Tuesday-night meeting was ask a question I borrowed from Assembly of God minister Dick Foth. He was a significant Christian voice on Capitol Hill in Washington, DC, to our nation's leaders. I had heard him lecture several years earlier on the theme of revolutionary Christianity. In that lecture, Foth shared a personal, life-changing experience that resulted from his meditation on one question: What did Jesus do with his time while he was on earth? I suggested that our group engage in a similar exercise. It took us a couple of months of reading through and discussing the four

Gospels, but we compiled a list of observable behaviors in which Jesus engaged.

- 6 percent of the Gospel's verses captured Jesus in prayer.
- 8 percent described Jesus healing and performing miracles.
- 8 percent showed Jesus confronting judgmental religion.
- 9 percent depicted Jesus breathing comfort.
- 9 percent captured Jesus simply answering questions.
- 11 percent pictured Jesus being with the marginalized.
- 20 percent portrayed Jesus talking about the kingdom.
- 29 percent presented Jesus showing followers how to replicate his works.

As we formed this list, something started to birth in us. The idea of behavioral Christlikeness sprang to life. Our list gave us something to use to compare our time use with Christ's time use.

We soon recognized that our version of Christianity consisted of a values-based list of activities rather than a behavior-based list. Our discipleship goals were wrapped around memorizing the Scriptures rather than practicing the works of Christ. No wonder our neighbors did not know us as they would know Jesus; we were doing completely different things with our time. For example, Jesus spent a good portion of his time with the poor; we never did that. He found it natural to breathe healing upon people; we would never consider praying for someone's healing unless it was in a Sunday gathering. New Testament scholar John Dominic Crossan observed that Jesus spent most of his time healing and eating, noting that if the average Christian just committed to those two practices, a vibrant expression of Christ would arise in them.[2] That idea confirmed our new vision and served to push us toward a far better expression of Christ than we had been presenting for many years.

The cause of our cancer was becoming clear. Thankfully, the cure was becoming clear too. A new sense of Christian spirituality began to fill our Tuesday-night meetings, and each of us committed to rethink our daily schedules to leave room to engage in the works of Christ. While doing the works of Christ seemed scary for most, it was at least clear. We now knew how to leave our consumer cancer behind; a new vision of Christlikeness had replaced our old idea of being saved.

A Fruitful Church

With a new vision for our personal lives in our hearts, it was time to talk about a new vision for our church. We started by acknowledging that our anemic version of Christianity had infected our corporate expression of Christ—our church. After all, our church was a collection of many individual expressions of Christ offered together as events, programs, organizations, and initiatives. Thus, if our individual Christians had cancer, then how could our church not have it?

Early in this second phase of confronting our cancer, I had a brutal moment of honesty. Church-growth pioneer Win Arn reported that eighty churches were closing in America each week.[3] And we were shrinking in attendance at a rapid rate. I figured out how long we had before it would become financially impossible for us to keep the doors open. The death date for our church was November 2011. I sat back in my chair and pondered that realization.

Then it came to me: we didn't have a theology of church closure. Further, I had never talked to anyone who did. Instantly I knew that was what our Tuesday nights needed to be about for the next weeks.

Where does one start to find a theology for church closure? And why did I feel so strongly that we needed this information? Something in me yearned for the reason why churches thrive, but I sensed that the best way to discover this was to first understand why churches die. Maybe it was a morbid thing; maybe it was a God thing. Frankly, I wasn't sure. But I committed us to the quest. I don't remember asking our leaders for permission; I just did it.

Somewhere between the discussions with our leaders and an inward discussion with myself, a familiar parable jumped off the page as I read it. It was Jesus' story about the unfruitful tree:

> Then Jesus told this story: "A man planted a fig tree in his garden and came again and again to see if there was any fruit on it, but he was always disappointed. Finally, he said to his gardener, 'I've waited three years, and there hasn't been a single fig! Cut it down. It's just taking up space in the garden.'
>
> "The gardener answered, 'Sir, give it one more chance. Leave it another year, and I'll give it special attention and plenty of fertilizer. If we get figs next year, fine. If not, then you can cut it down.'" (Luke 13:6–10)

For the first time in my life, I read this parable as an instruction for the church—Jesus expected his churches to be fruitful. In fact, he would do anything to make them fruitful—he would give them time, he would prune them, he would fertilize them, and he'd even dig around their roots. However, if a church continued to be unfruitful after such interventions, he would actually remove them from his garden. Could this be the theology of church closure we were looking for? Suddenly, I saw our Seattle church in this parable. Jesus had been waiting, and pruning, and fertilizing, and digging around our roots for years. And now we were starting a downward slide toward closure.

Armed with this parable, I made my way into our next Tuesday-night meeting, along with my leaders, to interpret and apply the parable to our church story. We concluded that for us, unfruitfulness meant the inability to rescue the lost. We admitted that we had no viable redemption plan in our church that worked, one that everybody knew how to engage in. We had been unfruitful in evangelism for some time. The odd thing is that I, as the pastor, had a gift for evangelism, and yet, I had found no effective redemption plan for our group. It had been a long time since we had brought in a lost sinner from our community, much less converted someone from the self-directed life to the Christ-directed life. We had won back a few prodigals to the faith who had walked away earlier in their lives, but we had demonstrated no skill in converting the sinners who lived all around us.

One would think that the weeks spent studying our demise would be depressing. Actually, it had the reverse effect. It was really nice to have a theology of church closure and to know exactly how the cancer had eaten away at us: we were statistically unfruitful. It was even better to know exactly what our Lord expected us to do so he would not be forced to remove us from the garden himself. That may sound brutal, but it was clear. And compared to the fog bank we had been in, clarity was appreciated.

We knew our next leadership challenge: we had to become effective at evangelism—to stop at nothing to become fruitful in converting the secular population that dominated our city.[4] While it would be a tall order for a traditional church like us to leave our deep history to become fruitful with Seattle's seculars, we realized that Jesus expected it! A sense of excitement filled our hearts. We had learned how to defeat cancer in our personal Christian expressions; we then saw how to defeat it in our corporate expression of Christ.

Our Tuesday nights took another turn; it was time to find a new way of doing church so we could take seculars to heaven. So, we took hold of hands all around that room and poured our hearts out to the Lord of the harvest, asking him to show us how to bring in this field. That prayer would change us more than anything we had done before. It turned us on to a completely different path.

Publishing Our Going-out-of-Business Date

The time had come to tell the congregation of the breakthroughs we leaders had experienced. Yet, we sensed the gravity of the challenge. We decided to level with them and publish our going-out-of-business date: November 2011.

I had delivered tough news to congregations in
my previous years as a pastor, but this news hit like a
sledgehammer. I still remember the looks on faces to
this very day. Some congregants were shocked; others
cried; still others sat with stoic, stone faces; and some
just closed their eyes and nodded their understanding.
Our honesty had required great boldness from our
leaders, but it was immediately rewarded.

A very certain and sober response arose from our
church family. We had feared that many would head
for the door like rats leaving a sinking ship. What we
saw instead was a group that was not only willing but
also determined to look for a new vision for our future.
The proof of this came when we called a special business meeting after a Sunday morning service to tell
them that we did not know what our future should
look like and that other urban churches had provided
little direction for us. Our challenge was unique, we
explained, because of the disproportionate secular
population of our city compared to other big cities in
the country.

After setting the backdrop, we laid out our options.
We could (1) glide into the night and thank God for
eighty-five years of ministry as we gracefully closed our
doors; (2) move out of the city into a suburban neighborhood with more families and serve the Lord there; or
(3) call a season of research and development and find
a new future for ourselves by trial and error. Within
twenty minutes, the entire church voted to engage
the season of research and development. Then, in a
bold move, they voted to borrow against our building
as much money as we needed to fund this research-
and-development season up to $500,000. This was the

meeting where our whole church caught traction and committed to a future that none of us understood. It was then that I started referring to our group as "the boldest church in America." And I still stand by that analysis.

Reinvesting Our Inheritance

The Lord had given us significant success over the decades, and our people had cooperated with him to create a wonderful story for Jesus in Seattle. We had a deep and abiding knowledge of the Lord, a history of boldness, property, and a will to be fruitful again in our city. We felt much like a young man who received an inheritance from his father that was earned from "old money" ways and now must reinvest that gift by establishing "new money" ways. We had a lot to work with that was passed to us by our sacrificial predecessors, but we now had to learn to reinvest that gospel capital in a new way for our city. We were blessed, to be sure, but we were also confused. Nonetheless, we had an iron will to not waste our inheritance, and we had a plan to cut through the fog and find a new future for our people.

Failure and Laughter

The next chapter of our church was filled with failure and laughter. We utterly failed at several different approaches to restore our fruitfulness. We tried serve teams, late-night Communion, citywide service events, and other initiatives. The only two rules we applied in our "return to fruitfulness" efforts were: (1) it could not be on a Sunday morning and (2) it could not be on our church campus. While many of our "reaches" were very popular, they only drew the already-saved. So, because they failed to reach the sinner, we declared them ineffective and canceled them. Then we would move on to the next test.

Our congregation was extraordinarily peaceful during this season; their bold faith was sustaining them. It was common for one of our people to stop me in the lobby after a Sunday gathering and say, "So, Pastor, what stupid idea bombed this week?" I would then recount our latest disaster, and everyone within earshot would circle around to listen to my report from the front lines and laugh raucously at the details of our miserable failures. This lobby drama occurred several times over those research-and-development months. But it always ended up with the encircling group patting me on the back and saying, "Now, don't give up!" It was truly paradoxical how our stories of failure were so enjoyable for our church, and yet beneath the laughter was a strong commitment to find a new tomorrow. I simply could not have been prouder of a church during those unstable and foggy days. It is an unbelievable blessing for a pastor facing an impossible challenge to suddenly see that God has flanked him or her with a bold people. My church was BOLD!

A Still, Small Voice

One failure after another visited us, and we were no closer to an effective redemption plan than we were two years earlier. We just had a growing list of what *didn't* work. Between these evangelism tests, something started to happen in me. I began to hear a soft little question in my mind: *What about the agape feasts that the early apostles used?* The inner voice would dull when we got ready for the next test, but would softly speak again after each failure. It was like a small splinter in my mind that I could not pull out. The idea of a dinner table–style church was so primitive that it seemed ill fitting for one of the most cosmopolitan cities in the country. Also—and I am embarrassed to admit this—it didn't require a performance-based ministry, so I ignored it. I had put many years and a lot of training and money into becoming an effective communicator and leading a Sunday worship gathering, but these agape churches were so simple that significant up-front leadership was not needed. So, I drowned out that still, small voice—until there was nothing left to try.

Adopted by a Vision

My wife and I rented out our suburban house and moved into an apartment in the city so we could learn about the people we were called to reach. Then we started our dinner church test in a community room a few hundred feet from our apartment. We set up nice tables with table cloths and started serving a full-course dinner, accompanied by our musicians singing worship songs, our artists painting sketches from the Gospels, and our pastors speaking a short message based on the stories of Christ. Within six weeks that room filled up with strangers and sinners who would never come to our Sunday gathering, yet were willing to sit with us, eat with us, become our friends, and talk about Jesus. We thought they would leave after dinner but before the preaching, but they did not. This was so unexpected, and it was so beautiful.

I remember the night it dawned on me that we were watching a miracle. It was a warm, autumn evening as my wife and I walked home from another dinner gathering. Suddenly, I announced that I sensed this was our future, that this was a vision of the new Westminster. Very quietly, she said, "I know." Sinners actually wanted to be with us, and the gospel was being preached to lost people. It was the first glimpse of a cancer-free future.

That was the night the dinner church vision adopted us!

THE FIRST DINNER CHURCH

He took some bread . . . broke it in pieces
and gave it to the disciples, saying,
"This is my body, which is given for you.
Do this in remembrance of me."

—Luke 22:19

The dinner church is nothing new. In fact, the dinner church approach to Christian gatherings has a rich theological heritage. As I studied the early Eucharist meals, I realized that the early church did not participate in these dinners as a spiritual practice, as we do when taking Communion. Rather, it was their way of doing church.

God Present at Mealtime

The dinner table theology, commonly referred to by theologians as "divine hospitality," is sprinkled throughout the Old Testament in a variety of celebrations and festivals. From the beginning, God showed up at mealtime. We see this clearly in Exodus 24:10–11 when God called Moses and the elders to come to Mount Sinai to ratify his covenant with them. While they were there, God provided a "divinely catered meal" that revealed an "unprecedented level of fellowship" with him.[1] We see it again just before Israel's entrance into Canaan, where God "spread a table" for them in the wilderness (Deuteronomy 29:5–6). The sacred meals of the Abrahamic covenant, the Sinai covenant, Gideon's covenant, and the many, repeating feasts of the Mosaic law had less to do with a covenantal signature and more to do with God being among his people and proving it by sitting down at a meal with them. The idea of God's presence at a sacred meal permeated Israel's mind-set such that these mealtimes reassured them that God was with them and intended to pour favor and blessing upon them.[2]

Jesus' Dinner Table Strategy

No one demonstrated a commitment to the dinner table theology as much as Jesus. It was against the Old Testament backdrop of sacred meal symbolism that Jesus shared table fellowship often, even with notorious sinners.[3] In fact, Jesus employed a very intentional dinner strategy during his three-year ministry. As stated earlier, an average day would reveal him doing two things repeatedly: healing and eating.[4] Correspondingly, the visual art of Jesus in the apostolic era reveals that the two most common elements of his life were shared meals and healed lives.[5] Jesus clearly employed a dinner strategy in his ministry— something that actually created many conflicts for him. At times, Jesus angered people because he extended a welcome to sinners and their friends to join him at his table (Luke 15:1–2). Most theologians now agree that eating with sinners was "one of the most striking marks of Jesus' regular activity." It is quite obvious that he intentionally made the open dinner table a central feature in the Christian tradition he was instilling in his followers.[6]

Jesus' dinner approach had a practical side. Most people worked during the day and were only available at dinnertime to engage in a spiritual conversation. But there was more than mere practicality involved in Jesus' use of mealtime; he viewed these dinners as an invitation to faith.[7] The Zacchaeus story is a great example of the power of a dinner table to usher in salvation. Jesus said nothing directly to Zacchaeus about his life, but the Lord's willingness to be with him, eat with him, and share life with him changed Zacchaeus's heart (Luke 19:1–10).

Dinnertime Was Story Time

Where did Jesus tell many of his parables? We may reasonably assume that the context in which Jesus usually recited these stories was during his controversial suppers.[8] In fact, Jesus seemingly crafted many of them to defend his practice of welcoming sinners to his dinners (Luke 15). Most New Testament readers have acknowledged that Jesus was a master storyteller, but have not imagined the dinner setting as the place those stories were told.

It is easy to see how these parables would captivate a roomful of listeners as they sat around tables of food. In fact, many of the parables were food and feast related

because of the setting and the invited guests. Once during
a dinner, Jesus instructed the hosts to invite the poor
and those who could not pay them back (Luke 14:12–14).
Then there's the most well-known banquet parable of
all, that of the Great Feast (Matthew 22:1–14). These
stories about inviting the poor to meals, banquets, and
end-time feasts reveal that Jesus saw that the kingdom
was best explained in terms of feasts and feasting.[9] A
final story that intensifies Jesus' charge to include the
poor at our tables is found in Matthew 25:31–46, where
he talks about separating the sheep from the goats. The
story ends with the door to heaven opened only to the
sheep—those who, among other things, invited the poor
to their tables.[10] Jesus' eating with sinners and telling
his stories about "the least of these" (v. 45) became the
common memory for the first followers of Christ.

Jesus' Vision for Church Gatherings

The greatest demonstration of Jesus' commitment to the
dinner table was the way he served the final Passover
meal. Jesus had gathered his disciples for one last dinner
before his arrest. When he lifted up the bread and the
wine and applied them to himself, it spoke volumes to
the disciples: Jesus was the Lamb who takes away the
sins of the world.

When he went on to instruct the disciples to share
that same meal often, and to remember him as they did
(Luke 22:19), it is very unlikely that they would have
interpreted his words to apply only to the bread and the
cup, as in modern church practice. We need only to look
at what they did following Jesus' ascension to know that
they embraced the vision of the whole meal that Jesus

gave them at the Last Supper (Acts 1:6–11; 2:42). After all, they had watched Jesus' dinner strategy for three years; obviously, they understood the vision he was casting during their final Passover meal with him.

In other words, the disciples were given a call to eat dinner with sinners and talk about Jesus. This was to be the manner of Christ's new church—a dinner church. The disciples caught the vision, and their gatherings were conducted in the likeness of the Master's: around tables at dinnertime. But to fully understand the vision of church that was cast that day, we have to understand the background of the Passover meal while Jesus was implanting the vision into those disciples.

The historic theme of the Passover meal was all about the rescue of slaves. When Jesus took that moment to launch his vision for the manner of his church, he forcefully connected his meals to the rescue of the lost and needy. The meaning of the Passover table was profound: God has rescued us and now sits to eat with us. Amazingly, Jesus instructed his followers to take that same table and its rich meaning of rescue and divine inclusion to the commoners, the sinners, the lost, the poor, the lonely, and the despised. The backdrop of the Passover is the greatest theological explanation for the dinner church, and from that spiritual history Christ instilled his dinner vision in the hearts of the first followers.

There was something very winsome about these dinners, because they had elements that worked against exclusion on the basis of one's poverty or even criminality, and instead included everyone at the same table as equals.[11] The meal vision that Jesus cast exemplified the radical leveling that ensured everyone would be served equally.[12] Jesus' life and his continual welcoming of slaves, sinners, and despised tax collectors made it impossible to imagine that Jesus would champion any meal setting except an inclusive, "come one, come all" dinner table. This, then, reveals why Jesus selected the Passover meal to launch his vision for how his church should gather and function.

The Dinner Vision and the First Church

Shortly following Pentecost, there developed a regular, weekly, common meal held in the house churches. By the second chapter of the book of Acts, the followers are going from house to house, sitting with their neighbors, breaking bread, and talking about Jesus. Whenever we see the phrase "breaking bread" it is speaking of a whole meal.[13] Immediately, the meal strategy of Jesus became the meal strategy of the first church, and can be seen all through the book of Acts and beyond. In fact, many New Testament verses make more sense when applied to a dinner table. A great example is the debate over whether or not it is permissible to eat certain foods, especially meat (Romans 14:2–3). The conflict was intense precisely because Christians were worshipping around the same tables at which they ate, and the meat in question was sitting right in front of them.

Many obvious references to the dinner church practice require no explanation, like when young Eutychus fell from the upper window as Paul preached right through the dinner hour. After Paul prayed for him, the believers all went back inside and finally ate, even though it was past midnight (Acts 20:7–11). We also see a dinner church gathered in Corinth (1 Corinthians 11:20–22). We know the poor were present because Paul was rebuking the wealthier Christians for hoarding the food. One of the later references that reveals a bit more about the dinner church practice is found in Jude 12, where the suppers were called "love feasts" (ESV) because it was the church's practice to recite Jesus' command to love one's neighbor as oneself while at the table.[14] Unlike Paul's epistles, which were written to specific places, such as Corinth and Ephesus, Jude's letter was written to many churches in the region—to be circulated and read by them all. Thus, it was clearly assumed that the agape meal was the typical manner of Christian gatherings, and the dinner church was already going strong in Bithynia by AD 113.[15]

It is worth pointing out that the ability to serve dinners and engage in hospitality became a stated requirement for leadership (1 Timothy 3:2; Titus 1:8). Hospitality was revered as a special mark of fitness for leadership within the household of God.[16] Obviously, that mark of leadership would not be important unless the practice of the group was that of a dinner church and focused on the needs of the poor, and the ability to serve the poor was not optional for those early Christians.[17] This was a dinner church, and its people were called to reenact the table of Jesus whenever they gathered.

Jesus was the greatest evangelist this world has ever seen. So, his gatherings would be effective in evangelism, too, or he would probably not be interested in their continuance. Accordingly, his selection of the dinner table as a strategy and primary vision for his followers reveals his belief that it would be effective at soul winning. The dinner table approach created an opportunity for easy and natural evangelism. The sharing of meals, which began with Jesus and continued throughout the New Testament era, was an ongoing feature that significantly helped the cause of evangelism right up to and beyond the end of the Roman Empire.[18] Some theologians go so far as to state that the growth in the earliest churches was wholly dependent on the meals and hospitality of the believers.[19]

There remained a natural draw for sinners to sit with saints, and while eating together, to talk about Jesus. Something wonderful, unexplainable, and transformative occurred in the hearts of the unlikeliest of people in these settings. And to our great surprise, we found the same ease of evangelism at our Seattle tables as was chronicled by the early church and the two-thousand-year-old dinner table tradition started by Jesus.

3

REBIRTH

"A man prepared a great feast and sent out many invitations. When the banquet was ready, he sent his servant to tell the guests, 'Come, the banquet is ready.' But they all began making excuses. . . .
"The servant returned and told his master what they had said. His master was furious and said, 'Go quickly into the streets and alleys of the town and invite the poor, the crippled, the blind, and the lame. . . . Go out into the country lanes and behind the hedges and urge anyone you find to come, so that the house will be full.'"

—Luke 14:16–23

Feeling the rich history of the dinner church at our backs, our congregation struck out to reenact the ancient fellowship meal approach to Christian gatherings. As with our many other tests, we hoped that this one might become a viable redemption plan for us, but after waves of failure we were not holding our breath. However, within a couple of short months, it became obvious that this dinner gathering was an effective redemption plan. It then became a divine call, and quickly became the central expression of our church.

A Written History

Not only did we have the scriptural evidence of the dinner table theology, as discussed earlier, but we also had access to many early church writings. Ignatius, the pastor in Antioch, wrote about his table churches in AD 115, and how their rooms were alive with a sense of thanksgiving and joy.[1]

At the end of the second century, the great champion of the dinner church was Tertullian, who wrote extensively about his agape feasts in North Africa. These evenings, he said, were filled with feasting, worship, singing of hymns, fellowship, concern for the lowly, care for the needy, and prayer for the sick—all of which was carried out under the Father's watchful eye.[2] The people would go forth from the feasts, not as mischief-doers or vagabonds, but as people who had just been to a school of virtue.[3] Tertullian intentionally located his agape churches near busy lanes so that people who were walking to the pagan clubs and taverns would see that the agape dinners were a richer and more rewarding fellowship and turn in to join them instead.[4] So, not only were the saved present; so were the poor and the pagans.

At the beginning of the third century, Minucius Felix wrote of how the feast churches were conducted with both a sense of gaiety and chaste conversation.[5] Then in the fourth century, Chrysostom spoke of the dinner churches in Antioch. Though they were not wealthy people, they cared for three thousand widows, prisoners, sick, and disabled people each day.[6]

The dinner church that started with Jesus became a house church among the Jews, and then became an agape church among the Gentiles. The dinner church approach was the dominant expression of church until Constantine made Christianity the state religion and changed its form to match the grandeur of the Roman polity. Though the Roman church leaders tried to stop the dinner churches because they did not follow their form or use ordained clergy, it wasn't until AD 692 at the Council in Trullo that the final vestiges of it were stamped out.[7]

Replicating the Ancient Way

We combed through these early church documents to develop a historic understanding of both the dinner table theology and their practical approaches. With those ancient voices behind us, we crafted an outline of necessary components for ourselves if we were to function in the likeness of the ancient dinner churches of the apostolic era. We would need to:

- locate them in a place and at a time that would allow sinners to observe our fellowship and feel comfortable to join us;
- provide a sumptuous feast free of charge to communicate a generous gospel;
- assure that everyone eats together—server and served, rich and poor, saved and sinner;
- sing Christ-focused worship music;
- preach from the Gospels;
- offer prayers for favor, presence, and healing; and
- maintain a prevailing atmosphere of Christ in the room of peace, joy, healing, and laughter.

These observations of how the ancient dinner table churches functioned were enough of an outline for us;

we simply repeated their template and started. After eight years of doing dinner churches in multiple locations throughout the city, and observing many other dinner churches that have sprung up in other cities, we have not changed a thing. The approach of old still works today—even in the most secular city in the nation.

Sociological Honesty

Once we decided to implement the dinner church, it was time for us to understand the sociology of our city. Serving as a pastor of a proclamation-based church had made me a theologian, but not necessarily a sociologist. The discipline of missiology is the equal blending of theology and sociology. While I knew our city needed the gospel, I did not know where the front doors to the city were located. The suggestion of the proclamation church was, "If you build it, they will come." I already knew that was not true; we had built it and they were not coming. So obviously, the front door to the city was not on our property.

Taking a page out of Tertullian's writings steered us to research the high-traffic areas of Seattle. After observing the movements of city people and spending time with some urban experts, we realized that the high-traffic areas of cities are their high-density walking villages. These restaurants, coffee shops, clothiers, and bars are surrounded by many apartments and condominiums in the stories above them. These locations create a sociology where people park their cars, take their walks, and catch their buses; the sidewalks come alive with people getting off of buses and walking to the many eateries.

We realized that these bustling walking villages were actually the front doors of the city, and a weeknight dinner church would see hundreds of people walking right by *our* front doors. Further, these were the locations where the strangers and the marginalized were. In fact, these walking villages were usually surrounded by sore urban elements and many deeply challenged people who were desperate for a place of peace to sit down and a family to welcome them. Who is better at being family than the followers of Christ? And what better way to provide a place of peace than a sumptuous dinner table? These high-traffic neighborhoods were the front doors of the city and would welcome our gospel— a gospel modeled by a big neighborhood dinner table.

A Surprising Birth Pain

Some of our rebirth pains we expected, like the pain of changing our worship gatherings or moving from our sanctuary. But there was one birth pain we did not see coming. In fact, our rebirth came a bit backward—we saw the *what* before we saw the *who*. That is, we saw the vision of the dinner church before we saw the social circle that the Lord would give us.

Jesus told a parable about a great banquet (Luke 14:16–24) to help leaders understand a very important *who*. In the parable, Jesus used a real event that actually happened and that had become a repeated story in the oral tradition throughout Palestine.[8] In the actual event, a king named Bar Maayan invited his people to a feast, as a sort of peace offering over some disagreements. But the invitees were still mad at the king and refused to come. It is interesting that the king controlled his temper and did not punish his subjects in some way, as he had full authority to do so. He simply reached out and invited commoners into his great hall, and then he invited some lower subjects, and finally even some of the vagabonds who lived along the hedgerows, until his great hall was full. This story had rippled its way through the land because the idea of the rich including the poor was rare. So, when Jesus used it, everyone knew he was retelling an event that actually happened, and it delivered a serious punch to the listeners who were sitting at that dinner table that night, and who regularly ignored the poor.

While reading this great banquet story one night, it hit me that the banquet holder's approach was perfect for any church that was in decline and whose house was not full. If Jesus were a good leader, he would certainly leave some instructions behind for his church as to what to do if they start losing influence. These *were* those instructions: any church whose ministries are becoming empty should start reaching for people who are a step down on the socioeconomic ladder. Then, if that church still has resources, they should reach down to yet a lower step, and even a lower one, until their house is full. Through that parable we felt as though Jesus were speaking directly to us.

But this was no small birth pain for us. We had always been a middle- to upper-class church, so our crowd leaned toward well-to-do people. So, to apply the instruction of the great banquet story meant we would have to make a shift in our identity. But we were losing influence, and we were shrinking, and we now saw this story was directly for us, so we took a deep breath in our spirits and humbled ourselves to serve a lower populace. We had seen the *what*, but now we beheld the *who* of our future—the "least of these" (Matt. 25:40). And guess who started walking into our dinner church rooms at a ratio of two to one? The poor, the broken, and the displaced. We wrapped our arms around them and called them family. And that is exactly what churches are supposed to do.

Those Who Came

The early church writers reported that they filled up their rooms with strangers, sinners, the sick, and the poor. That same cross section of people was the first to fill up our rooms as well. After opening up eight sites and measuring the crowd at the one-year point, we noted that (1) one-third of the attenders are financially challenged, with about half being homeless and the other half being the working poor; (2) one-third of the attenders are isolated, most of whom are second-life singles—those who have already ruined one life and are desperately hoping not to ruin another; and (3) the good Samaritans who live in the neighborhood, most of whom are millennials, join with the Christians to befriend, serve, and lift everyone else in the room. That has become the milieu of our dinner churches.

There is usually an ethnic minority that commonly dominates each neighborhood, and this becomes visible in our rooms too. In one dinner church, it is African Americans, in another it is First Nation peoples, and in yet another it is Hispanics. It is an unspeakably beautiful thing to see a room full of different ethnic backgrounds all eating together, talking together, laughing together, and praying together. The homogeneous unity principle

(HUP) of "birds of a feather flocking together" simply does not apply at a Jesus dinner table church.

A Different Kind of Leader

The next lesson in our rebirth process was discovering what leadership needed to look like to make a table church thrive. These were not outreaches; they were churches that needed a pastor who felt called by Jesus to take personal responsibility for the Christian spiritual development of the people. So, we re-tasked our staff to drop their previous roles and, instead, begin spending a day a week in their neighborhood, using coffee shops as their offices—pastoring the sidewalks by day and leading their dinner church that night. Most of our staff had enough of an evangelist call to make the shift, though some left for more traditional positions. Our pastors served as overseers of the dinner gathering, especially the other team members, such as musicians, cooks, servers, security personnel, the Samaritans who showed up to help, and the missionaries who showed up to breathe encouragement at the tables. Our culinary staff began cooking up a storm, our musicians put worship sets together, our artists set up easels and painted gospel metaphors on canvas while people ate, our pastors preached the Gospels, and our Christians started seeing themselves as missionaries to certain Seattle neighborhoods. It was a beautiful thing to watch people self-assign and find their individual places of service in meaningful roles.

At the very beginning of our dinner church chapter, I told the Lord that I was exhausted trying to find volunteers to fill the positions for our Sunday church, and that I certainly did not have the energy to enlist and train enough volunteers to sufficiently staff our dinner churches that were spreading throughout the city. I sensed the Lord speak to my heart that I would never have to ask for leaders or volunteers; he would send them to me. Honestly, I doubted that I had heard the Lord correctly, but I agreed to go forward.

The Lord of the harvest was true to his word; I have never sought to enlist a pastor or made a call to get a volunteer to show up. We now have enough lead teams for seven churches, and they have all come to us because they felt called by the Lord to be there.

An Evening at Dinner Church

If you were to attend one of our dinner churches, you would walk into a room of cloth-covered tables, set up for approximately one hundred people. There would be a buffet table loaded with colorful food including potatoes, gravy, vegetables, a huge salad, carved meat, bread, and a good dessert. The food would be served by a friendly line of people, names would be remembered, and everyone would be treated like family. The worship musicians would be playing and singing something you might expect to hear on a Sunday morning, the artists would be painting at lighted easels, and conversations at the table would be punctuated by the occasional outburst of laughter. Sitting at the table, you might be surprised by the diversity of those eating together—proof that truly everyone is welcome in this place.

At some point during the evening, the music would stop and a pastor would preach on a story from the life of Christ. Then the pastor would pray a generous prayer for Christ's presence, healing, and favor to descend upon every person in the room. The entire speaking and prayer portion would be less than ten minutes.

If an artist has finished his or her painting, that individual might take the mic and explain what he or she was reading in Scripture or feeling in prayer when the image on the canvas came to mind. That is always a very intriguing part of the evening. Then the musicians would resume their worship music, and the people at the tables would go back to talking among themselves. It is at this point when the Christ-followers tend to experience their richest conversations with their friends. Conversations about life often lead to discussions about Christ, and sometimes lead to one-on-one prayer right at the table. The worship music and table conversation continue to the end of the evening.

Many times, I have stood to the side and just observed the spiritual movement occurring in the room: someone being prayed for by a Christ-follower, another person sitting quietly and wiping away tears as the worship music is sung, yet another laughing because he is enjoying the only family he has in the world, and a single mother with two children leaning over their second plate of food because it is the best meal they have had all week. At those moments, I remember Jesus' story of the great banquet and note that it is occurring again right before my eyes.

Feeling the Spirit of the Lord literally washing back and forth over the heads of strangers, sinners, and broken people is sometimes more than I can emotionally handle. I am often filled simultaneously with joy and tears—joy because this Great Commission environment is allowing Jesus to gather his sinner friends, and tears because their lives are so broken. But to walk and work in the great banquet rooms of the Savior is an honor—without equal.

When we look back to what we were ten years ago, it is painful to see how ineffective our church was in the rescue business, but exhilarating to remember how far we have come. Because this historic church decided to revisit the ancient dinner church vision, we know full well what redemptive flow feels like. We are a church reborn!

4

PREACHING TO SINNERS

In the beginning the Word already existed.
The Word was with God, and the Word
was God. . . . So the Word became human
and made his home among us.

—John 1:1, 14

Before we could ever be effective as a church, our understanding of preaching had to go through a rebirth season. I had been preaching several times a week for twenty-seven years, and frankly, I thought this would be the easiest part of the transition from the proclamation church to the dinner church. But I was wrong. In truth, proclamation gatherings are statistically only effective with Judeos—those who already have a churched set of values—and my preaching had been steered by the maturity of the crowd. Dinner churches, however, are Great Commission environments in which the room is full of seculars and sinners, and I had not preached to that kind of crowd. So back again we went to the apostles' template and discovered that their version of preaching was focused solely on the stories of Christ and the stories Christ told. We forget that they did not have a Bible, like we do. In fact, the New Testament was being written as they went about their ministries. I am sure they never imagined that their letters and writings would one day be bound together to become the approved Holy Scriptures. The only informational tool they had to work with was the life of Christ. Paul revealed that single focus quite clearly as he declared that when he preached, it was about Christ and him crucified (1 Corinthians 1:23). So, they told and retold the stories of Christ, and by those messages and teachings they built the first church.

Preaching the Christ Stories

One of the greatest proofs that the apostles focused primarily on the Christ stories is the presence of the book of Mark. John Mark was not an eyewitness to the life of Christ; he was too young. However, he was able to read and write, so he took notes of Peter's preaching in his mother's upstairs flat (which was probably the first church in Jerusalem). If it was an average Jewish house church, then approximately forty-five people gathered each week, and it was there that Peter instructed them in faith. And what did he talk about? He simply repeated the stories of Christ. The book of Mark was Peter's preaching content, nothing less and nothing more. That is why some of them are out of order; they were not intended to be a sequential history document, but an example of the early apostles' preaching. It is the simplest book in the entire Bible. You can read a section of Mark and almost hear Peter finish preaching and go into a prayer. The etymology of the word *preach* comes from the Greek *kerygma,* which apologist and priest

Michael Green argued is the recounting and restating of the simple stories of Christ.[1]

When we realized that the apostolic preaching that filled the early dinner churches was actually the simple recounting of the stories of Christ, we had to admit that our staff had never actually preached; we had only taught. That was quite a shock for me personally. I guess I felt that to earn my salary I needed to punctuate a scriptural section with exegesis, hermeneutics, apologetics, and compelling illustrations to create a spiritual thesis that was worthy of the many hours put into its creation. That was not kerygma; that was teaching. This is likely the reason churches are not seeing more salvations: pastors are trying to teach their way into sinners' minds rather than kerygma our way into their hearts.

Kerygma is not about information; it's about Christ's story intersecting with the listener's story; it's about relaying a divine invitation to people who aren't used to Jesus talking to them. The scripture that helped us most with this insight was "faith comes from hearing, that is, hearing the Good News about Christ" (Rom. 10:17). Like most Western Christians, we interpreted the Word of God to mean the written Scriptures, the Bible. But as I stated earlier, the first Christians had no singular and bound written manuscript to work from, so how did they hear Paul's words? By holding to the first rule of interpretation—let Scripture interpret Scripture—we found ourselves in John 1, where we read, "the Word became human and made his home among us" (v. 14). That added a lot of clarity to how those first apostles understood the Word of God: it was Jesus. Those two verses created a huge breakthrough moment for our leadership team.

The Divine Invitation

We now understood that faith was birthed in sinners' hearts solely by kerygma. Teaching was still valuable, but the divine invitation that birthed faith was only served by the stories about Christ—simple retellings of the stories of Christ.

Martin Luther must have had a sense of this, because he insisted that when his leaders read from the Gospels, they stop talking after the reading, to let the truth of it settle in the hearer's heart.[2] (He did not require this after the reading of any other portion of the Scriptures.) It became obvious to us that the apostles understood something that our pastoral team and I did not. We understand it now.

There is a reason so few seculars find Jesus during Christian preaching: we are not actually *preaching*. The stories of Jesus are not the focus; the divine invitation is not actually happening. Well, that was our turning point. Once we were willing to put away our polished and well-trained teaching skills, we were able to offer the simple stories of Christ, and the divine invitation began to flow night after night. Though we were totally unimpressive to our pastor friends when they would visit, we were successful in helping our sinner friends see Jesus and hear him invite them into his kingdom. It was now a whole new game. Our new approach was a divine invitation, followed by a prayer that invites Jesus' presence, healing, and favor to descend into the room. With this simple preaching approach, there is often such a feeling of favor in the room that applause breaks out spontaneously at the end of the prayer, and this from people who would never have imagined they would be in a church, listening to a pastor, a year ago. But that is the power of the divine invitation.

Christianity versus Churchianity

We did not expect to find much interest in the gospel when we entered our first neighborhood in Seattle. We believed the sentiments of other frustrated church leaders, that Seattleites were simply not interested in Christianity anymore. Our assumptions turned out to be wrong—way wrong. We found surprising interest in the person of Jesus. There may not be equal interest in debating doctrine, or religious instructions, but our tables revealed significant interest in talking about Christ. Once we started limiting our speaking themes to the stories about Christ, agnostics, Muslims, Hindus, and almost everyone in the room started listening.

Our original assumption was that most would eat and then get up and leave. We had printed up table tents explaining that there would be a Christ story and a prayer offered at the end for those who wanted to stay; we wanted to alleviate any bait-and-switch feeling among our first attenders. But to our great surprise, almost everyone stayed, even though they were done eating. This became especially true once the attenders realized that we weren't trying to merge them into a Sunday church gathering somewhere. It was not uncommon to have five people eat and leave, to intentionally skip the speaking and prayer portion. However, after a few months of attending our dinners, even those people started staying through the speaking and even bowing their heads during the prayer.

To this day I am shocked at the interest in the life of Jesus that is commonplace in our city, the most liberal city in the United States. I have come to this conclusion: the average secular is fine talking about pure Christianity; it's *churchianity* that they don't like.

Worship Music for Seculars

The use of music to focus people on the Lord and prepare hearts for the Word has been foundational in Christian worship for centuries. However, we didn't see how that was going to fit in our dinner churches, even though we believed it to be a critical component. As in most traditional churches, worship for us had been a stand-up singing experience. But we were now faced with seculars and sinners who didn't sing. So, the question for us was: How do we use the power of music and the call to worship without asking the group to join us?

We soon discovered that upper-tempo music did not create the same peaceful atmosphere in the room that Christ-focused, reflective music did. So our musicians needed to grow their list of moving worship songs so as to last through an hour set, especially the songs that talked about Jesus. They quickly shifted, and now you'll hear the most worshipful thing you'd ever hear on a Sunday morning throughout the hour. The instrumentation is usually a guitar or an electric piano, and sometimes there might be a conga drum or a drum box backing up the worship leader, which is appropriately simple for a dinner room. Our worship leaders quickly realized it was their role to usher in the presence of Jesus. It is not uncommon to see people push their plates aside, close their eyes, and let the worship music wash over their tired souls. We have come to realize that while seculars don't sing, they will sit and wipe away tears while you sing.

Sermons on Canvas

Another form of preaching that developed in our story was the use of canvas art. This is the only component we added to Tertullian's outline. While painted images about many of Christ's stories are present in the frescoes and the catacomb art in those earliest centuries, there would have been no easy medium for it to be brought into a dinner room. Nonetheless, the art of the day had a strong Christian association. Much of the art that informed Leonardo da Vinci and other Renaissance artists was taken from the artists in the apostolic era and their imageries of the crucifixion, the resurrection, the feeding of the five thousand, people being healed, Jesus at dinner tables, and many more scapes of the Gospel stories.[3]

For us, the idea emerged right up front to use live painters each evening to paint sermons on canvas about the stories of Christ while people ate. We thought it would engage people who were unfamiliar with the Scriptures in a visual way, one brushstroke at a time. This idea really caught momentum when we considered how many painters the Lord had already placed in our midst, and they became immediately excited at the opportunity to use their artistic talent for evangelism. Several of them stated that they had felt a tug in their hearts to consider the ministry, but they could never see themselves as speakers. Now, however, the idea of preaching with brushes, colors, and Jesus-images was deeply meaningful for them.

We started to loosely refer to these paintings as "kerygmagraphs" because they were as much a part of the telling of the Christ stories as the pastor's verbal message on any given evening. And true to our antici-pation, the crowd became intrigued by the developing image; our artists were, indeed, preaching on canvas. Often people would stand around the artist as he or she painted and ask what the painting meant, how he or she first got an image in mind, and the reasons for partic-ular color and genre decisions.

Many times over the years, a child has been drawn close to the artist, only to have an apron put on him or her and the artist to put a paintbrush in the youngster's hand and teach the child how to paint a Jesus story of his or her own. It is amazing to watch a parent who is observing his or her child paint a story of faith, while ten feet away a musician is singing music of faith, and an entire room is drawn into the mentoring moment. Through our live canvas art, Jesus' influence is seeping into so many hearts and in so many different ways that it is incalculable.

No More Preaching to the Choir

Preaching, in whatever form, is an indispensible component of the gospel; no one can draw any other conclusion in the light of the Great Commission. However, the Reformation template initiated an environ-ment that then created a speaking form that is limited to "preaching to the choir." In other words, the procla-mation church assumes that everyone in the room is a

Judeo with a basic respect for the church sociological construct. This form of preaching was developed at a time in which Europe was completely Christianized, everyone was getting a copy of the Bible for the first time because of the invention of the Gutenberg printing press, and the Protestant churches were founding their gatherings to teach their people how to be the priests of their own homes.[4]

Five hundred years later, we are still using the same preaching form that the reformers did, though the missiological climate is now much different. While it might come as a surprise, it is not the way the apostles preached. The dinner churches of old were environments in which the Christ-stories flowed naturally from the apostles as people ate and listened. If we are going to use the church form of the apostles, it might be wise to use the preaching form of the apostles as well. We have never second-guessed that decision.

THE HEALER

[Jesus] noticed a man with a deformed hand. . . .
Then he turned to his critics and asked,
". . . Is this a day to save life or to destroy it?"
But they wouldn't answer him. He looked around
at them angrily and was deeply saddened by
their hard hearts. Then he said to the man,
"Hold out your hand," . . . and it was restored!
—Mark 3:1, 4–5

We made another unexpected discovery the first year of doing a dinner church: just because Seattle was not interested in attending a Sunday church, it did not mean they were not interested in talking about Jesus— including his healing. The stories of Jesus' healings were too numerous to ignore in our preaching, so we told them. We were hesitant at first because we had considered healing to be one of those topics best left for the mature Christian crowd, or a special day like "Healing Sunday," but the more we preached through the Gospels for our secular friends, the more we realized it was not a ministry that Jesus reserved for the mature followers. In fact, it seemed to be a lead activity of his. So, we got over the fear that it might be asking for too much faith from faithless people, and started boldly retelling the stories of healing. And to our surprise, the crowd listened. They did not jump up and tell us we were crazy, nor did they ask for us to heal them, but they did listen. The stories about healing created a sense of wonder, and wonder is one of the soulish ingredients that can turn into hope, then faith, and finally, prayer. While it took some time, these accounts of Jesus' healings started to matter to our people. We soon found people were not only willing for us to pray healing prayers for them; they started asking us for it if we weren't quick to offer it.

Sinners and Healing

We have noticed that the theme of healing feels more natural with sinners than it does with many Christians. Those who have been in the faith for a long while tend to have some baggage attached to the idea of healing. Some have been embarrassed or frustrated when they prayed for healing and nothing happened. Others have heard teachers explain that healing is a limited grace that is reserved for those with the gift of healing, or that it is something that God only gave to the first apostles so they could plant the church. Still others have connected it to primitive Pentecostal expressions, such as snake-handling, and have thrown out the baby with the bathwater on the topic. Then there are the believers who have lived in this rational-based world of modernism for so long that, while they believe Jesus did it, they don't think it is likely to happen today. For these reasons and more, many Western Christians do not make room for healing.

I would offer another reason most Christians do not engage in prayers for healing: they have not been given a chance to practice it. Most Christians attend churches that are teaching environments that offer no place and space to engage in healing prayer for needy people. Further, praying a healing prayer for someone at work or school would be totally unnatural, as these are secular environments. So where would the average American Christian ever practice such a thing as praying a healing prayer for someone whose life sorely needs it? This is where the dinner church shines; these rooms are Great Commission environments that are filled with broken and hurting people who know they need a Physician. And these rooms are places where Christians can naturally practice all the works of Christ—including healing.

Broken People Need Healing More than Others

There is another point to be considered here: many Christians enjoy a rather comfortable lifestyle and simply do not feel the same desperation for the Healer's touch as does the lower third of the population. Most of our churches are located among the middle- and upper-class neighborhoods across the country; thus it is difficult for most Christians to imagine how the lower third live, how their lifestyle diminishes their health, and how truly limited their options are to deal with health care issues. Their limited finances mean they have poor insurance coverage, if they have any at all, so if they have to choose between going to a doctor or feeding their kids, they will choose the latter. So, they develop chronic issues in their lives that they just have to live with. This is normal for the lower third. Consequently, when this population walks into a dinner church and hears about a healing Jesus, it strikes a different chord in their hearts than in the majority of our suburban Christians; they feel a degree of desperation for the Healer that is not shared with the upper tiers of society. This is a sociological reality that makes many who attend dinner churches more open to the topic of healing—because they truly need it.

A Natural Fit

As previously noted, to observe Jesus would be to mostly watch him eating and healing.[1] For us to practice the Christlikeness of eating naturally led to us to practice the Christlikeness of healing. With that growth of understanding, we worked to make our dinners places where people could talk openly about their challenges, brokenness, and sicknesses. It is amazing how willing people are to talk about sore-life issues when they know there is a Healer in the room. Further, once brokenness was verbalized, the next obvious step for our Christ-followers was to stop and ask the Healer to visit them. In this way, our dinners and healing became a natural fit, like a hand in a glove. A dinner church cannot engage in Christ's activity of eating without engaging in his other primary activity of healing. The call to invite the Healer into people's lives is now a call that we take seriously, and even expect. After practicing these healing prayers night after night for eight years, rare is the dinner when we do not pray for at least one person for healing, nor is it uncommon to hear people report back on how things changed after the healing prayer. Dinner and healing is a match made in heaven—literally.

Healing Is Not an Event

The theology of healing needs to be reconsidered by any group that is considering doing church in a way that creates a Great Commission environment. Many shy away from the practice of healing because they are afraid that if they pray for someone and nothing happens, they will be left having to explain why to a disappointed subject. That reveals a very shallow understanding of what healing is about.

Healing is not an event. Let me say that again so it has a second chance to soak in: healing is *not* an event. Healing is a relationship with the Healer, Jesus. When we pray for someone at one of our dinner tables, we are not asking for an instantaneous fix; we are asking the Healer to come into the individual's story and start to breathe healing into his or her situation. The emphasis is on the Healer showing up, not on how or when he is going to fix something. It is up to him to select how and when the healing will come.

Scripture introduces Jesus as both the Savior and the Healer (Isaiah 53:5). It is interesting to me how people can so readily accept the Savior showing up in their lives and cleaning them up, but then stumble at the topic of the Healer showing up in their lives and restoring their strength. Jesus is the same Lord, whether showing up as the Savior or the Healer. When salvation is needed in people's lives, we pray for the Savior to flow into their story, and we have faith that he is doing his work. Similarly, when sickness and brokenness are apparent, we should pray with the same confidence for the Healer to flow into their story. When we approach healing prayers in the same way we approach salvation prayers, it should be a natural thing that doesn't create an odd, mystical expectation to wait and see if those for whom we have prayed "feel" anything.

Praying for the Healer to show up is a far greater prayer than asking for a healing. Healing is situational, but walking beside the Healer has a multitude of ongoing impacts in our lives and those we are praying for. Practicing the presence of the Healer is a wondrous thing, and showing our friends how to practice walking beside the Healer is a doubly wondrous thing. I invite you to recognize the deeper theology of healing: start inviting the Healer into people's broken situations, and expect him to be good at his job and walk into their lives with healing in his hands.

Simple, Quiet, Healing Prayers

The prayer that invites the Healer does not need to be a profound spiritual experience where the organ is playing, the elders are laying on hands, and a deep, mystical feeling marks the moment. While that form of prayer is certainly honored by the Lord, it was far more common in the life of Christ for the prayer of healing to be done in a simple, natural way that was consistent with the environment in which it was being offered. The healing prayers that our dinner church pastors and Christians pray are simple, quiet, one-on-one prayers that are offered while sitting at tables. It is done so unnoticeably that most other people at the table do not even realize it is happening. This form of tableside prayer is something anybody can do. In fact, so simple are our prayers for healing that we find non-Christians even praying the prayer of healing for others.

One day my wife was approached by a lady who referred to herself as an atheist with a spiritual dilemma. She told Melodee that her apartment manager had cancer and thought he needed prayer, so she wanted to know how she was supposed to pray to a god that she did not believe in. Melodee sat down and wrote out a prayer for her neighbor. I'm sure you can see that that woman was not far from the kingdom of God. In fact, within the year she introduced herself to one of our new pastors as a Christ-follower. The simple tableside prayer this woman had observed was such that she felt she could do it for a sick neighbor.

If the Healer is paying attention to all of our lives, then anyone should be able to invite him into any story, and he will come. We believe in the simple tableside healing prayer that anyone can do. No chanting, no organ, no elders, no humming, no swaying, no group laying on of hands, no voluminous cries—just a simple invitation for the Healer to flow into a person's body and painful story. That is a prayer of healing that fits the environment of a dinner room, and it is more powerful than many Christians can ever imagine.

This past December I was sitting in a coffee shop, and one of our dinner church friends was sitting at the next table. I called him over and, as we talked, he shared how frustrated he was that his friend was not working on kicking his heroin habit. He went on to say that he himself had kicked heroin that past year, but his friend would not even try. I asked him how he had gotten free from it, and he looked at me with one of those "you've got to be kidding me" looks. He then pointed at me and said, "You guys got me free." I asked him how that could be true because none of us even knew he had a problem with the drug. He then told me that every time the heroin voice would come into his head, he would start making his way toward whichever neighborhood we had a dinner church in that night. He said, "All I had to do was ignore the heroin voice until 5:00 p.m., because when I got around you guys, and you started talking about Jesus and praying, the heroin voice would go away." After three months of bringing the heroin voice into our room, he was free. Our simple healing prayers that were offered in natural and small ways were working in him in big ways, and we did not even know it!

A couple of months ago, a woman I'll call Adrianna, from one of our downtown dinner churches, met me at the door when I walked in. She was in her late sixties and had lived a very renegade life. She told me that since she had been hanging around our dinners, she had become increasingly intrigued about Jesus.

While at home one night, she decided to risk it and turn on a Christian TV show, in which a lady from Texas was talking. In the middle of her message, the speaker stopped and said, "There is someone listening to me that has a back injury, and Jesus wants to heal it. So, I want you to stand up right now in your house."

Adrianna, who'd had a back injury, yelled at the TV, "I am not going to stand up for you." But the speaker kept insisting she stand up. "It's like she knew I wasn't standing up and was not going to stop asking until I did," she told me.

Adrianna finally did stand up, alone in her house. Then the speaker told her to bend over and touch her toes. At this point, Adrianna told me, she said some "not very nice words" to the TV screen, because of how much pain that would cause her. But after another round of insistence, she did bend over, and for the first time in over a year, there was no pain. And, in fact, her pain has been completely gone since.

Then she looked at me and asked, "Okay, pastor guy, is that what they call divine healing?" I said yes, that is what it was. She replied, "So, Jesus looked into my room, saw my back injury, and spoke to some preacher lady in Texas to tell me to stand up and touch my toes to prove that he had healed me?"

After laughing with her at the patchwork explanation of events, I told her that Jesus had been paying attention to her throughout her entire life, not just that night. When I said that, her eyes began to fill up with tears. She uttered a four-letter word and said, "No! Really?" Then she went over to Melodee and said, "Your husband just told me that Jesus has been paying attention to me throughout my life. Is he telling the truth?" She also approached two other leaders and asked the same thing. Of course, they all confirmed the attentive presence of Jesus. Adrianna just cried. The ways that healing works in a Great Commission environment are unlike anything many Christians have ever experienced.

Healing and Salvation

Historically, there has been a significant correlation between healing and salvation. Throughout the Gospels it is evident that Jesus used healing as a way to demonstrate the love of God, and then invited those he healed into the kingdom of God. One of the last things Jesus said upon the earth before ascending was that his followers would do greater works, healings, and miracles than even he did (John 14:12).

The first apostles and leaders obviously took that to heart, and stories of healing flooded immediately into the pages of Acts and the Epistles as a natural activity of their Christian expression. True to Jesus' prediction, stories of healing have been commonplace throughout the centuries of Christian history.

Today, much of the Western church has been overly affected by rationalism, and the theme of healing has been placed on the back burner. Christ's approach of using healing to open the door for the kingdom of God has almost completely fallen from our practice. Presenting Jesus as Healer as an evangelism strategy is not usually considered in missional planning meetings.

Pentecostal pastor and adjunct seminary professor David Lim reported that almost 100 percent of people who find Jesus in Africa experience healing first, 30 percent of people who find Jesus in Asia experience healing first, but less than 3 percent experience healing before salvation in the West.[2] It is not that the Healer is being inactive in our part of the world; it is simply that our Christians are not asking him to show up.

More Prayer; More Healing

David Godwin, who is a leading missionary in my denomination, was very effective in presenting the Healer first, then the Savior, during his work in Panama. One of the primary lessons he learned about healing is that the more you do it, the more healing occurs. So, he started compelling Christians to pray the healing prayer anywhere, everywhere, whenever one has the chance. While healing will not always happen right then, it is something that increases with practice. Truthfully, almost everything in Christian discipleship must be practiced into existence. Why would healing not work the same way? Many Christians have acknowledged that walking with the Savior has become more meaningful with practice. Similarly, David proposed that working with the Healer becomes more effective with practice too. So, we direct our people to pray the healing prayer whenever the opportunity presents itself in our dinner rooms, until it becomes an effective part of one's Christ-expression. The future of the dinner church will be impacted by how practiced we are in praying for healing to descend into our rooms, and how continually we look for opportunities to invite the Healer into the lives of our unsaved friends.

The Frustrated Healer

There is a Gospel account where Jesus met a man whose hand was deformed from birth (Mark 3:1–5). In most settings Jesus would have simply healed the man and moved on. But this was the Sabbath. Judgmental Pharisees were watching, and they would consider it a breach of Sabbath law for Jesus to heal on that day. Jesus asked them if the Sabbath was a day for doing good deeds, or for doing evil. He then asked if it was a day to save life, or to destroy it. But they remained silent. Jesus shot an angry glare at the Pharisees because they were so uncaring, and then healed the man. Notice with me how frustrating it was for the Healer to be told he was not allowed to heal (Mark 3:5).

In some ways we, as church leaders, wondered if Jesus had ever felt a similar frustration with us. We were here to represent Jesus, who was the Healer, but we weren't inviting the Healer into the needs of our guests. Back in the proclamation phase of our church, this did not seem to be such a big deal, but now, in this dinner table phase of church, we realized there were far more people who truly needed Jesus to show up for them. We needed to step up our practices of healing in this new Great Commission environment. While we weren't being pharisaical, we were frustrating the Healer nonetheless.

I still remember the moment when I was alone in prayer and said out loud, "Okay, Lord, I will stop shying away from healing and will start actively looking for opportunities to pray the healing prayer." The next week, I stood before our church and told them that we had all invited Jesus *in*, but it was time to start letting him *out*. And if we are going to let him out in our dinner churches, he is going to come out *Friend* for the lonely, *Savior* for the lost, and *Healer* for the sick. So, let's go let him *out*! Following that directive, I watched a significant upswing in one-on-one prayers being offered through our rooms. I daresay that the Healer has not been nearly as frustrated in our rooms from that time on.

THE MESSAGE OF FOOD

"I stand at the door and knock. If you hear my
voice and open the door, I will come in, and
we will share a meal together as friends."
—Revelation 3:20

A meal that is served as a Christian expression is different from a group of people eating together. When studying through church history, the closer we get to the first church, the more we find the idea that having a meal with Christian purpose was to have a meal with Christ.

Food Can Be Sacred

The divine table fellowship idea spilled over into Israel's daily life. "The practice of hospitality in the ancient Near East, going back long before Jesus' time and continuing to today, involved the notion that the guest in someone's tent or house was sacrosanct, treated with respect."[1] The late Brennan Manning, author of the famed *Ragamuffin Gospel*, stated, "The ancient Jewish practice of inviting someone for dinner meant, 'come to my *mikdash me-at*,' the miniature sanctuary of my dining room table where we will celebrate the most sacred and beautiful experience that life affords—friendship."[2] Hospitality was a divinely inspired activity for ancient peoples, and it always involved shared meals and validated the dignity of guests.[3] The people who were most affected by Yahweh were drawn to value the sacredness of mealtime.

Jesus' use of food and dinnertime created the expectation of immanence. It would be wrong to assume that gathering for dinner was merely a church model. For the first followers it was the way they embraced the promise of God's presence among them. "The Qumran texts bear witness that in some quarters in early Judaism, Messianic hopes were high, and meals were seen as one essential part of the *koinonia* that one would share with the Anointed One."[4] In other words, though they predated Christ's arrival on the earth by a couple of decades, their meals were rich with anticipation of the Messiah's presence. The Qumran community, like the early church, saw these meals as an anticipation of the final banquet with Christ in heaven.[5]

The early disciples experienced numerous connections between suppertime and Christ's presence. For instance, the meal that Jesus gave to the disciples of bread and fish on the shore after Jesus' resurrection signifies not only the appearance of the risen Jesus, but his abiding presence at his called mealtimes.[6] Then there was the time when Jesus met the two on the road to Emmaus. When he sat to eat dinner with them and broke the bread, their eyes were opened (Luke 24:30–31). These instances and more led those first followers to understand that any Christian supper was a sign that Jesus was still among them.[7] I imagine that Christ's final words, "I am with you always, even to the end of the age" (Matt. 28:20), rang the loudest in their hearing as they sat together at their agape feasts because they knew he was sitting there with them.

The power of a Christ meal to open up a portal between heaven and earth is immense and important for us to meditate on. In the light of the rich history of God showing up at mealtime, we have the ability to actually create a Great Commission environment that brings Savior and sinners to the same table to share life together.

Lessons from a Family Table

The evening dinner table was a big deal for the Fosner family. When we think back over the high points of our family's time together, it is at the top of our list. Our evening tables were filled with colorful and thoughtful menus because Melodee nurtured our family from the kitchen. Even though our meals weren't always elaborate, they communicated attentiveness from the heart of "Mom." Dinners were an event where we lingered. The evening wasn't just about the food, though; it was what happened around the food that created depth in our family. There was sibling banter and meaningful conversation, laughter and tears, contemplation and reaction, blame and apology, regret and celebration. Our dinner table was the paradox and a mosaic combination of happenings; it was the best expression of our beautiful, imperfect family. This brings me to lesson one: around food, love can flow.

Beneath it all, Jesus was there. Most Christians understand the omnipresence of God, but there is a difference between knowing God is present and feeling his stirring in the soul. We experienced the latter at our table—a lot. We took turns praying for the meal: sometimes it was soulful, sometimes it was quirky, and sometimes it ended with laughter. And I am sure Jesus was laughing with us, though it sometimes bordered on sacrilege. There were other times when our conversation led to a revelation of a very sore soul, one that called for me to put down my fork and lead the family to the Healer, or the Provider, or the Leader, or the Savior. Tears would flow, hugs would follow, and the family would regain our strength in each other and in the presence of Jesus. This leads to lesson two: around food, church can happen.

Our dinner table was a place where other people often joined us. Though many of these guests came from very different backgrounds, it was only a matter of minutes before we were all enjoying conversation and laughter. Though we were people of faith, some of our guests were not. Though we were a healthy family, some of our guests came from unhealthy situations. Though we were a loud and laughing group, some of our guests were introverts. Yet, it never ceased to amaze us how quickly people who were so different started to enter into our family bond. And in the space of a couple of hours around our table, which wasn't unusual, we would hear the most interesting revelations about their lives, their stories, and even their regrets. Some people we had known for years became completely different people at our table as they told us stories from their pasts that we did not know. Over and over again, acquaintances became family right in our dining room. Lesson three: around food, barriers come down.

One morning while in prayer, Melodee saw a picture of five strong towers that she knew was an image of our family. She started to talk about that with our kids and pray that over us daily. Soon, that vision of strength became a shared image that we all drew strength from. It was never scripted or coerced, but it flowed naturally out of Melodee and me. We talked about attitudes that made for strength, practices that made for strength, prayers that made for strength, and friends that made for strength. The vision of those five strong towers shaped us all. I will forever bless my wife for offering that imagery that flowed into our dinner table and into our hearts. This is lesson four about dinner tables: around food, the future can be shaped.

If your family lived on a deserted island with no other people, how would you do church? Can you imagine doing it any other way than around your dinner table? Whether a biological family of five, or a neighborhood family of 150, it works quite the same. The simple way Jesus worked at our family table gave us an understanding of how to work with him in one of his dinner church tables. In fact, it became a very helpful filter that protected the simplicity of our dinner rooms; if an idea was more complex than we might do at the table with our own families, we nixed it. The genius of the simple family dinner table became our template and formed one dinner church after another.

Evangelists Who Cook

Moving from a traditional church that spent most of its time in talking events to a church that would spend most of its time in meal events created an unexpected opportunity for us: our culinary people could now use their skills in evangelism. The idea of cooking meals that went directly to influencing the lost brought many people to the surface with great excitement.

An abundant buffet table was the best way for us to reveal an abundant gospel and a generous God. That talk infused meaning into our cooks, and they started creating the primary metaphor for the kingdom of God night after night. This was a different form of cooking than anything they had done in their church kitchen before; this was evangelism. In fact, I started calling them evangelists when I walked through one of our kitchens, because it was an accurate depiction of the work they were doing.

On a practical note, our food plan has always been simple. We pick up the food at a restaurant supply at noon, start cooking it in a community center kitchen, have it ready to serve by five o'clock, and have it all gone by the end of the meal—even if that means putting it in to-go containers. Leaving nothing to wrap up, store, and refrigerate makes for simplicity during the breakdown. The number of people and the alignment of cooking teams has taken on many forms over the years and through different sites, but the pattern of buy fresh at noon, serve at 5:00 p.m., and have nothing left over by 6:30 p.m. has remained.

The typical meal consists of a large salad; a vegetable dish; a starch; an entrée, such as carved meat or lasagna; bread; and a dessert. Sometimes a community space does not have an adequate kitchen, so we cook at our central kitchen and transport the food to the site in a hot box. This is both quicker and easier than most people imagine. We serve all hot food off of chafing dishes. This gives the buffet table a catered look, and chafing dishes are easy to work with for a team setting up and tearing down a room. To serve someone food, and then sit with them and eat with them, is a wonderful experience for both the church and the guests.

Closing the Distance between Heaven and Earth

God uses the metaphor of food and dinner too many times for us to ignore. Could it be that our Lord chose the dinner church vision with an eternal message in mind? A Jesus dinner table connects the spheres between the natural world and the supernatural one. The two disciples on the road to Emmaus experienced the Lord in a divine and unexplainable way while they ate together. Recently, a lady said to my wife, through tears, "When you guys look at this, you see a community dinner; when I look at it, I see life. Jesus has to be so proud of you." Somehow, when she held her plateful of food, she saw Jesus. That is eerily similar to the Emmaus story.

Many Christians would long to be in places where they could see the door open up between heaven and earth. Celtic Christians used to ask each other if they had been to the "thin place" lately. The thin place for them was where the veil that separates heaven and earth became so thin that people could actually see God walking and hear God speaking. While that question has not been asked among most American Christians, there is a desire to be in a place where we can gaze into God's world.

While these divine portals have commonly been explained as existing in the spirit, I might surprise you by saying they also exist locationally, on the earth. There are certain places and events that Jesus inhabits in more voluminous ways than others. A Jesus dinner table among the poor is one such place. Dick Foth used to say, "If you have lost Jesus, go the poor and they will lead you back to him."[8]

Jesus unapologetically gives preferential attention to the poor, and when we are serving a dinner to them, it can't be explained any differently than a portal opening between heaven and earth. There we are actually working beside Jesus in healing, serving, touching, caring, embracing, offering comfort, breathing courage, and inspiring faith. Christine Pohl, speaking of her own experience, stated, "I discovered just how heavy large pots of soup could be and just how precious it was to share a meal with a lonely person."[9]

There are thousands and thousands of American Christians who are in need of that same precious discovery; they need to know where to go to see into the activity of heaven. Every time we eat an agape meal with the poor and the lonely, we are experiencing yet another opening between heaven and earth.

TABLE TALK AND NATURAL EVANGELISM

*There was a man . . . named Zacchaeus . . .
[who] had become very rich. He tried to get a
look at Jesus, but he was too short to see over
the crowd. So he ran ahead and climbed a
sycamore-fig tree . . . When Jesus came by, he
looked up at Zacchaeus and called him by name.
"Zacchaeus! . . . Quick, come down! I must be
a guest in your home today.". . . But the people
were displeased. "He has gone to be the guest of
a notorious sinner," they grumbled. Meanwhile,
Zacchaeus stood before the Lord and said,
"I will give half my wealth to the poor, Lord, and
if I have cheated people on their taxes, I will give
them back four times as much!" Jesus responded,
"Salvation has come to this home today."*
—Luke 19:2–5, 7–9

We did not know how to talk to seculars and sinners
over dinner, and there was no value in denying it. Most
of the people in our church had logged very little talk
time with seculars in a relaxed, sit-down environment.

Like most Christians, we had spent our "Jesus time" with other Christians, where every conversation assumed a similar spiritual ethic. We liked the safety of not being asked to explain our salvation to someone who thought we were primitive or stupid. But, we were filling up our room with the very ones who brought us the most discomfort to be around. At first, our people instinctively hid themselves behind the buffet table and refused to eat, claiming they did not want to take food away from the poor. But that practice could not stand for long, not at a Jesus dinner.

Sequestered Christians

I remember some years ago traveling with a group of pastors to visit a church that served the poor. While we were there, I watched as those seasoned spiritual leaders sequestered themselves from the crowd one by one by slipping into the kitchen to engage in comfortable conversation with each other. It was as though the loneliness and needs in the dinner room with more than two hundred poor folks did not even exist. The leaders did not recognize what a tragedy it was that their knowledge of Christ and their love would go unshared that day. They also did not recognize the message of exclusion they were sending. But that is normal for sequestered Christians.

This is the reason Paul was so angry at the Corinthian church as they sat, eating up all the food, while the poor were left standing against the wall with nothing. His charge was that they were not discerning the body of Christ (i.e., they were not representing the body of Christ on earth) (1 Corinthians 11:22).

Christendom and the Reformation era interpreted that verse as not offending the holiness of Christ. However, in context, it appears that Paul's rebuke was more sociological: the exclusion of the poor is not the nature of Christ and should not be the nature of his church.

The historic nature of the agape feasts was informed by the nature of Christ, which assumed all kinds of people would be welcomed to the table and everyone would eat together as one big family. The answer was simple: we had to learn how to talk with strangers, sinners, and seculars.

Confession Is Not the Goal

Through a series of disappointing outcomes, we realized we needed to reconsider the path of salvation for the people the Lord was giving us. We had assumed that the Romans road was as good for them as it was for us, but those explanations hit an awkward tone. Further, like most of our brothers, we had lived in the Reformation era for so long that our first goal was to get them to confess their sin. The only problem is that Jesus embraced many people who did not confess anything first: he came to us while we were yet sinners (Romans 5:8); he was a friend of sinners (Luke 7:34); he saved a woman caught in the act of adultery when she did not even confess her sin (John 8:1–11); he proclaimed forgiveness to a prostitute who was washing his feet with no confession (Luke 7:37–48); and he invited himself into Zacchaeus's life and gave salvation to him after Zacchaeus merely offered to pay restitution to the people he had wronged (Luke 19:2–10). Jesus' path to salvation was obviously wider than the sinner's prayer.

In fact, Jesus recognized every gesture that moved a person closer to him.

Every Gesture of Faith

Our dinner church team began to pay close attention to every gesture of faith. When someone stayed through the preaching, even though he or she could easily have left, that now meant something. When someone paid attention to a Christ story, and even asked about it later, that meant something too. When someone bowed his or her head during prayer and welcomed the care, that also meant something. And when someone started talking about praying to Jesus, however simple, that now meant something very significant: that individual was starting to cooperate with Jesus in the navigation of his or her life. The Savior was now knowledgeably at work in the person's life—that is salvation. So, we learned to look hard for that gesture.

Some months ago, a man I'll call Mark started attending our Bitterlake dinner church. He was financially challenged, was a friendly sort of guy, but had erratic and loud mannerisms. Whenever the preaching started, he put his oversized headphones on and turned it up so loud that you could hear squeaks coming out. He would then pace back and forth, until finally he would walk up to the front of the room as if he were frustrated, noisily find a chair to sit in, and rock back and forth. It was so unsettling that the security guys would follow him around the room so they could stop him if his erratic behavior ever escalated. Though he never disturbed the preaching, it continued to happen for several weeks.

One day, I happened to stand beside him in the line to the buffet table, and asked him a question about his life. He motioned for me to hold still, while he riffled through his backpack for his headphones. I stood silent while he held up his pointing finger, until he got his headphones on and plugged them into his phone. Then he said, "Okay, go!" I stood there speechless as my mind processed what was happening. The man was mostly deaf, and his headphones with a phone app were the only way he could hear. All this time we were interpreting his pacing, his front-row rocking antics, and his headphones as a guy who was uninterested in the gospel and being disruptive, when in fact the exact opposite was true. He was so hungry to hear the preaching that he was willing to walk around the room to find a listening point that worked with his apparatus, and if that failed, he would pace to the front of the room and lean forward to get enough volume to hear what was being preached. This was a modern-day Zacchaeus story if I ever saw one. Everyone, including me, thought he was odd, but he was actually desperate enough for Jesus that he was willing to do socially abnormal things to hear about him. Just as Jesus discerned Zacchaeus's gesture of faith, we had to learn to discern the first steps of faith and interest in Christ. In fact, we are still learning it.

The classic understanding of grace is *prevenient grace* and *concomitant grace*. Prevenient grace is that which the Lord pours upon people before they realize he is doing it; concomitant grace begins when one starts to knowingly cooperate with the Lord in their ongoing salvation. Our dinner churches are prevenient grace environments in which Christ's favor is being poured upon people who don't know yet it is him. Sinners don't know what to do with this grace that is flowing, so they do all kinds of things. Some of the reactions are odd, but tucked behind the social abnormalities can be gestures of faith. We must discern these gestures. The path of salvation is far wider than we first believed.

A Surprisingly Painful World

Our dinner church tables were filling up with broken people with raw emotions, crass words, troubling stories, scary lifestyles, and painful pasts. We had to learn to not be shocked by our conversations with them. Most Christians have very sanitized lives. Our words are cultured, our home life is sheltered, and our ideas about life are incubated in a world of answers. This is not a shared reality with one-third of our population.

Stories of poverty, attacks, beatings, rapes, thefts, murders, and drive-by shootings became the talking points at our tables. One man's fourteen-year-old daughter was kidnapped by a south Seattle street gang who raped her throughout the night. When his sixteen-year-old son tried to intervene, the gang killed them both. The father found them draped over a tree limb the next morning.

I wish I could say that gruesome stories like this are rare, but no. Trivial answers, like, "Just pray," don't get very far in the raw world of broken people. We found we needed grace just to listen to their stories; then we honestly process their emotions with them, feel their grief, question God with them, and then go home with a prayer on our lips. But where else does Jesus want his presence? He wants us taking him to those who need a doctor (Mark 2:17).

Every decade or so, the world theological leaders get together to observe the progress of the gospel across the globe. They give a short overview of each portion of the world, for its positive or negative impacts on the global gospel. In 2010, after the world congress in Cape Town, South Africa, the paragraph written to explain the state of the gospel in America indicated that American Christians are far more blinded by their prosperity than they realize, and they have almost lost the theology of the sacrificial faith altogether.[1]

In a micro way, we realized our own congregation had lost the theology of the sacrificial faith, and if we were going to be meaningful in a room filled with broken people, we would need to observe the Scriptures in a new light. But that is why Jesus sent us there—because he is a friend of sinners, and he needed to use our bodies so he could be physically present at the table with them.

No Trump Cards Allowed

Another lesson we had to learn was to stop pulling our Christian trump card of truth. Jesus does not have us here to straighten out our dinner guests' thoughts and realign their lives, and it's a good thing, because their challenges are quite impossible at times. What Jesus needs most from us is for us to be their friends.

Truthfully, our Christian answers are not all that good for the world our dinner guests live in. Our theologies have been shaped from the safety of our sanitized suburban world, where most churches are located, and that perspective makes it difficult for us to easily observe the theologies of poverty and suffering. We had to spend

serious time in the Scriptures before we could offer
meaningful answers for our guests' harsh world. But
once we started eating with the dinner church crowd,
we began to see verses popping off of the pages as we
never had before. But even so, no trump cards allowed.

Let Them Lead

The fourth lesson we learned was how to let the guests
take the lead in the conversation. We noticed that
making friends with a stranger tended to follow similar
talking points. Further, we realized that if we let them
have the lead, they would deepen the conversation
when they were ready. The first level of conversation
is about life, theirs and ours. This level could be about
hobbies, happenings, things to do, and so on.

After a while, sometimes minutes and sometimes
months, they would deepen the topic from *life* to *limitations*. At this point, they would start talking about the
things in their lives that they could not change but wish
they could. We began to see this as a serious growth step
in the friendship, and we started sharing with them
our limitations and frustrations about the things in
our lives that we couldn't fix either. This was difficult,
because we had to resist the Christian reflex of putting
a faith statement after a limitation statement. But it was
necessary to stay at the level that we had been invited.

Finally, after a few discussions about limitations,
our guests tended to introduce the next talking point—
spirituality. They would start talking about Buddhism,
Universalism, marijuana, alcohol addiction, Higher
Power, their study of comparative religions in college,
and so forth. When those topics started to surface, we

realized we had just been invited into the deepest part of their souls. What an honor. To spend a good deal of time talking with them about how their spirituality works for them and how they got into it always paid good dividends.

Respecting people's spiritual answers is necessary for any friendship to survive. Somewhere in our conversation, there would come a time for us to talk about our spirituality, which is Jesus. To share how Jesus helped us with something would be welcomed because they had invited us into the spiritual level already. But let me hasten to say, we learned not to hog the conversations. In fact, to let them have twice as much time on their spirituality as we took explaining our spiritual stories is a good rule of thumb. The last thing we wanted was for a new friend to feel devalued by our words, and our use of conversation time communicated that we respected each person's answers and spirituality. By respecting the conversation, we were respecting our guests and honoring the friendships we'd made. Letting them take the lead and determine the level they wanted to talk on has allowed us to disciple our friends toward Christ, night after night.

A couple of years ago, a large group of young gypsies was coming through Seattle, saw the signs on the sidewalk, and decided to come in to one of our dinner churches. They were all traveling together in a nomadic way, both guys and gals, and one of them had a baby. Melodee has a mother's heart, and it compelled her to their table, where she began diving into their lives. They laughed about their clothes, talked about their musical instruments, and soon Melodee was holding their baby while they ate. Finally, the conversation turned to the festival they were headed to. It was called Wanderlust, which was a gathering for free spirits. Melodee asked what they did there, and they said that among other things they prayed and meditated. That was the invitation into the spiritual level, so Melodee asked the group, "Who do you pray to?" They started answering her with various answers, and she just listened. The conversation continued for some time. As they were leaving, Melodee asked one of the young men, "Would you consider praying to Jesus this time, and see what happens?" He promised to do so. And with hugs and wishes from Melodee, they were on their way. What began with talking about life, turned into talking about limitations, and ended with an invitation to pray to Jesus. But Melodee respected the level on which they wanted to talk, respected their answers, and ultimately gained the right to talk on the spiritual level with them.

Evangelism Is Easy

The ancient agape meal was the primary manner of evangelism for the early church. There remained a natural draw for sinners to sit with saints, and while eating together, they talked about Jesus. Those who gathered around those tables might have been sinners, but they were redeemed sinners.[2] Like the agape meals of the first three centuries, our meals have allowed us to observe that the sinners in our rooms are not only deeply loved by the Lord; they are sought by his grace, and the momentum toward their salvation is already started. They might be sinners, but the atmosphere of redemption is all around them. Over and again, when I look at a room of broken people, I hear the Lord whisper to me, *"They are mine."*

■ ■ ■

His name was Salvador, and he had moved to the United States from El Salvador some years ago. He was a homeless street performer who played his colorful conga drums for spare change on a corner near one of our dinner churches. Salvador spoke broken English and had warm eyes and a winsome smile. But he was also an alcoholic. He came for dinner every Wednesday night, and at the end of the prayer, he would startle the crowd with a thundering "Amen." Everyone in the room soon learned to wait for it each week. It was endearing.

Melodee started praying for him that the Lord would free him from his alcoholism. One night she made up her mind that, as she puts it, she was "going in for the kill." In other words, she intended to pray at the table with Salvador to be delivered. But as she sat down beside him, she felt the Spirit halt her and say, *"Melodee, I got him."* So instead of praying, she simply asked, "Salvador, you love Jesus, don't you?"

He looked at her with such reverence and said, "Oh, Melodee, how could I not? Look what he has done for me!" As it turned out, Salvador already knew Jesus. He did not meet the spiritual checklist that Christianity has held, but he already had Jesus, and Jesus had him. His boisterous "Amens" were not a drunk man following a form at all; it was a man communicating with his Savior.

Melodee settled in herself that Salvador might not be free of his alcoholism on this earth, but he would be free one day in heaven. While that kind of rocked our theology, it also freed us from feeling the need to serve the spiritual growth "list" and, instead, trust Jesus to be good at his job.

Salvador has since died. By the time of his passing, he had cleaned up, he was living in an apartment, and alcohol no longer had a choke hold on him. Turns out, Jesus was good at his job after all.

8

A DIFFERENT PATH OF SALVATION

"The Kingdom of Heaven is like a farmer who planted good seed in his field. But that night . . . his enemy came and planted weeds among the wheat . . . When the crop began to grow and produce grain, the weeds also grew. "The farmer's workers went to him and said, . . . 'Should we pull out the weeds?' . . . 'No,' he replied, 'you'll uproot the wheat if you do. Let both grow together until the harvest. Then I will tell the harvesters to sort out the weeds.'"
—Matthew 13:24–30

The dinner church vision took us out to the edge, where our rooms began to fill up with a different kind of people. We realized that these people the Lord was giving us needed a different explanation of salvation than the one that had been in our mouths for decades. So, we found ourselves looking for a different way of telling our new friends about our Jesus.

Seculars and Judeos

America is becoming predominantly secular. Only fifty years ago, it could be assumed that most Americans had a working knowledge of what went on in a Christian church. Today, the majority of our city's population has no one in their families who ever attended church, with the rare exceptions of weddings, funerals, or special events. In Seattle, only 5 percent attend church, and another 5 percent used to attend church, leaving a full 90 percent who have little experience with the Judeo-Christian worldview. Their worldview has been formatted by secular ideas; they are the New Gentiles. This changes the question for church leaders from, How do we retrieve the prodigals? to, How do we get the gospel ready for secularized people? Fortunately, the church has been at this intersection before.

One of the major themes of the book of Acts is the church getting the gospel ready for the Gentiles. The day the Holy Spirit came on Cornelius's house during Peter's visit, everything changed. It was now obvious that the gospel of Christ was intended to flow into the Gentile culture. However wonderful this was, it created a frustration for the birthing church, because Gentiles did not share the same history and values with the Jews. While Peter focused his ministry upon the Jews, Paul focused his efforts on spreading the gospel to the Gentiles (Galatians 2:7–8).

The Right-Wrong Explanation

Paul's first task of translation was to acknowledge that the Gentiles had a different starting point than did the people of Israel. The Jews were comfortable with a right-wrong approach to life because of their long history with the law of Moses, but the Gentiles were not comfortable with the presence of an authoritarian code. Aware of this cultural reality, Paul went to work disengaging the gospel from the right-wrong constructs of the Jews. This is visible in his comment to the people of Corinth that though all things are now "lawful" (KJV), they might not be beneficial (1 Corinthians 10:23). Later he spoke clearly about the law being replaced by the new covenant (2 Corinthians 3:11). To the church in Rome he stated that the only way to not be under condemnation was to have no law to break (Romans 4:15). When speaking to the churches in Galatia, Paul was frustrated that they were being "bewitched" by teachers who were leading them back into a right-wrong definition of the gospel (Gal. 3:1–3 KJV). He directed them to send the law away just as Abraham and Sarah sent away Hagar and the slave child (Galatians 4:29–31). These are only a few examples of Paul's efforts to dismantle the right-wrong construct for the sake of the Gentiles. He maintained the message of freedom from the law throughout his epistles.

In the book of Hebrews, which many believe was written by one of Paul's ministry partners, Priscilla, the right-wrong construct of the law is referred to as "obsolete" now that the new covenant has come (Heb. 8:13). These reductions of the right-wrong constructs that promoted authoritarian imageries were intentional and necessary in making the gospel ready for Gentile peoples. Michael Green has noted that even phrases such as "the kingdom of God" were not particularly helpful to the Gentile milieus, and terms such as "salvation" progressively became the replacement in the New Testament.[1]

Explaining the gospel in right-wrong authoritarian terms was at a cultural impasse with the Gentile populace.

The Grace-to-Grace Explanation

If Paul was not in favor of serving up the right-wrong construct to the Gentiles, what did his salvation path look like? Simply put, it was a path that erased the curbs of the law and replaced them with the presence of the gracious Savior. Paul's salvation was not based on human reasoning, but rather on the gospel of Christ (Galatians 1:11–12). To remove a right-wrong approach to life is not reasonable to many people, but the gospel of Christ can function without it nonetheless. Paul was well trained as a Pharisee, and he understood the power of the law to promote righteousness. However, on the road to Damascus, Christ told Paul he was persecuting the Way.[2] At that moment Paul experienced another transformation power—the personal presence of Christ (Galatians 1:15–16). Compared to his earlier commitment to transformation by the coercive law, Paul now embraced this different way of walking, and coveted that for all the churches under his charge (Galatians 4:19).

The law created curbs in one's life, so to attain righteousness one must maintain one's behaviors within the listed curbs—all 613 of them.[3] However, due to humanity's penchant toward waywardness, it is only a matter of time before one collides with the right-wrong curb of the law and feels the failure of the collision. This repeating certainty makes the path of salvation a condemnation-to-condemnation experience. However, Paul's instruction to leave the right-wrong curbs behind and, instead, start walking with the Spirit of Christ, turns one's path of salvation into a confidence-to-confidence experience. This manner of transformation makes room for a person to deal with the detriments in his or her life one by one, as the Lord sees fit. While some egregious things that the Spirit hasn't brought to the fore yet may be in a person's life for a long while, it is a gracious approach to transformation.

Three Gospels in Paul's Day

Paul's path of grace was not synonymous with the path of license. In fact, Paul clearly recognized that three approaches to Christianity were being attempted in his day: the *law gospel* by the Jewish Christians, the *license gospel* by the Nicolaitans and others, and his *grace gospel*. Throughout the centuries, many leaders have wrestled with the New Testament as though there were only two options: law and grace. This dual understanding has often led to error because it lumps all the scriptural warnings against the way of license into the grace category, causing the path of grace to become bloated by law-like language. But Paul's grace-to-grace presentation was a different path altogether, a third path to Christian development. For those who were bent on promoting a form of Christianity that did not assume transformation unto Christlikeness, Paul and the other apostles ruled it as the path of license, and found that the law was useful again for confronting their lawless intents (1 Timothy 1:6–11; Galatians 1:6–9; 5:19–21; Jude 4; and Revelation 2:12–25). Nevertheless, that was not the path of grace that he had painstakingly forged for the Gentiles.

Paul's grace-grace gospel not only fended off the way of license, but it also traded the curbs of the law for a walking relationship with the Spirit of Christ. Walking with the Spirit promotes a picture of being guided from one spiritual place to a higher spiritual place; it speaks to the progressive nature of our salvation. John used the phrase "grace for grace" to reveal this progression (John 1:16 KJV). Similarly, Paul used the phrase "faith to faith" to the Romans (Rom. 1:17 KJV), and to the Corinthians he said that we were being transformed into the image of Christ "from glory to glory" (2 Cor. 3:18 KJV). These state-to-state imageries reveal a way of walking toward our Lord's ideal for us: being guided from victory in one area to victory in another; from one place of strength to another place of strength; from one achievement of faith to another achievement of faith.

Of course, while dealing with one part of our life at a time, there must be time, space, and grace for areas not yet rescued. But this is what makes grace-to-grace such a beautiful replacement for the pervasive pressure of the right-wrong law to fix everything immediately or be deemed a transgressor. However, this slower approach to Christlikeness requires patience on the part of the church, and a strong belief that the Savior is really good at his job.

Christ's Surprising Instruction

Jesus told a parable about a farmer to demonstrate how to coexist with fallenness (Matthew 13:24–30). In this story the farmer planted some seed. Later he noticed there were weeds growing among his seeds. His workers assumed they would be pulling the weeds, but the farmer stopped them because the effort of pulling the weeds would dislodge the good plants. The farmer further told his workers that there would be a day when the weeds would be separated out, but not by them—they were only to nurture the good seed.

What a picture of working with sinful people who are making their way to Christ! It is not one of imposing a right-wrong construct, but rather one of offering grace for the weeds that persist, while nurturing the seeds of the gospel that are growing.

Paul understood this when he instructed the church in Rome to not pressure those who were buying meat that had been offered to idols, but rather offer grace for each person to work out the issue in his or her own way (Romans 14:1–13). With the churches of that day being dinner table gatherings, this meat issue was front and center every time they met. Yet, Paul's instruction was to offer grace and not nullify the work of the gospel over where one buys his or her food.

The New Covenant and Sin

The old covenant held a different definition of sin than does the new covenant. The law used "sin" to demarcate between righteousness and unrighteousness. A word study of the eight Old Testament terms for "sin" reveals a punishment-centric idea that is directly related to walking past one of the lines of the law.[4] The way of grace, however, uses "sin" in a completely different way. The New Testament's singular word for "sin" is a navigational term that is akin to veering off course from the heading that would lead to a port of blessing.[5] Thus, when Paul said that everything is "lawful" (1 Cor. 6:12; 10:23 KJV), he was not proposing a way of license, nor was he doing away with the transformational goals of the gospel. He was instead making room for the Spirit of Christ to navigate his people, step-by-step, toward a port of blessing. This simpler definition of sin as a navigation term could be made no clearer than Paul's encouragement to be controlled by the Spirit rather than being controlled by the lines of the law (Galatians 5:18).

For one to get off course and then be directed back toward a port of blessing by the Savior is quite different from hitting a curb of the law, feeling condemnation, and being bounced back into the "right." Paul longed for his people to experience a path of salvation that was laced with confidence rather than the pervasive feeling of condemnation (2 Corinthians 3:9, 12). While many Christians through the ages have felt obligated to blend together Old Testament law and New Testament grace (resulting in a confusing theological soup of grace and law), it must be noted that any spiritual path that uses punishment is different from what Jesus and the apostles held (Romans 8:1).

Why, then, would anyone avoid sin? Simple: sin leads people to a port that they will not like once they get there. Paul reminded the Galatians that every seed a person planted in his or her life would grow up to be a blessing or a curse (Galatians 6:7–8). The reason people avoid sin is that they do not want to experience a harvest of angst, remorse, and disappointment. While grace refuses to make criminals out of those who are headed in a harmful direction, it still works to steer them back on course to the port of their high calling. That is the new covenant way, and it is a beautiful thing.

The Problems with Penal Substitution

Today's Christians come by their sin-centric explanations of salvation for good reason. Five hundred years ago, during the Reformation, John Calvin created an explanation of atonement called *penal substitution*. Among its helpful qualities, it brought a few challenges into the salvation conversation, the greatest of which was the idea that those wanting to come to Christ must deal with the penal (punishment) part of their lives before they can gain access to the Savior. This courtroom metaphor made perfect sense to Calvin; after all, he was a lawyer. In his imagery of salvation, a person is charged, and the divine gavel pounds down, announcing that he or she is found guilty. Then, if the convict confesses his or her sin, Jesus will take that person's place and be hauled off in handcuffs, leaving the accused absolved and free to go home. To be clear, substitutionary atonement and penal substitution are not the same thing. The former is a scriptural idea that dates clear back to the practice of the scapegoat in Israel's history; the latter is a construct of Calvin by merging verses from the book of Romans.

The challenge is that this explanation puts inordinate pressure on the practice of confession. A simple study through the New Testament reveals that of all the times the term "confess" is used, only three of them are connected to confession of sin (Matthew 3:6; Acts 19:18; James 5:16). The predominant usage is that of confessing Jesus is Lord (for example, Matthew 10:32 KJV; Luke 12:8 KJV; Romans 10:10 KJV; Philippians 2:11 KJV; 1 John 4:15 KJV). Those are two very different ideas. While confession is certainly included in Scripture as a great salvific step, it is not the only way people begin their journey of faith. The church's obsession with confession as the change point from sinner to saint needs to be reevaluated. Even the sinner's prayer has only been practiced for 150 years.[6] Think of it: the church has helped people to heaven without the confession-based sinner's prayer for more than eighteen hundred years.

Further, note that when Calvin penned his penal substitution theory, Europe was completely Christianized.[7] Everyone was at church come Sunday; the only question was whether it was an Anglican, Catholic, or a Protestant church. Accordingly, there was very little missiological need for the reformers to explain atonement to beginners, as the assumption of church gatherings was akin to "preaching to the choir." While this explanation of salvation has served the church for five centuries, it is now creating confusion and frustration when used with the New Gentiles.

Getting the Gospel Ready for the New Gentiles

Throughout church history, whenever someone has steered the gospel toward an oppressive right-wrong construct, God raised up an immediate voice to call people back to grace-grace. When the first Jewish Christians assumed that the gospel would have firm laws in place, God raised up Paul. In the tenth century, when Anselm of Canterbury initiated the idea that God needed satisfaction from someone whenever he or she sinned, God raised up Abelard to remind the church that the active ingredient of salvation was love: Christ first loved us, and that causes us to love him in return. When Calvin pushed his penal substitution theory, which forced sinners to court before they could expect their Savior's intervention, God raised up Jacobus Arminius to proclaim that prevenient grace is only the beginning of Christ's marvelous waves of grace.

In recent decades we have watched the Neo-Reformed movement arise, complete with name-calling to guilt people back to lines, laws, and exclusion. These leaders who interpret Paul through eyes of justification on the basis of a few verses are overlooking his message of reconciliation, which is the dominant theme of his writings.[8] This view creates a backdrop to the gospel with hard edges and harsh tones.

Also in recent decades we have watched some strong Neo-Arminian voices arise and feverishly erase the right-wrong constructs that the Calvinists had erected. Even though some have gone too far and wandered off the end of Scripture, the church at large is still feeling obligated to hold on to a gospel with right-wrong lines firmly attached. While this might work for the already-saved, it excludes the majority of the American population. Thus, there is a need to win back a grace-grace presentation of the gospel such as the apostle Paul served to his people.

Should the bulk of the church persist in offering the right-wrong narrative, then every societal issue that comes along will be met with another wave of Christian leaders restating their stance, followed by another wave of seculars resenting Christianity. Sixty years ago it was women wearing makeup; fifty years ago it was dancing; forty years ago it was divorce; thirty years ago it was drinking alcohol; twenty years ago it was abortion; today it is the homosexuality issue; and tomorrow it will be something else. Dating back to the days of Paul, history has taught us that right-wrong answers exclude people and drive a wedge between society and the gospel. But grace-grace answers have historically gathered all kinds of people around a surprisingly warm welcome from Christ himself. And this is what it means to get the gospel ready for the seculars.[9] For such a call as this, I propose that my Arminian brothers arise: the New Gentiles need us!

The Different Path

Today we are eerily close to the place the first church found themselves. Christians are holding to an explanation of the gospel that they have rehearsed for five hundred years. And though it makes perfect sense to the insiders of the faith, it creates an obstruction to anyone who has been raised with secular worldviews. Black-and-white approaches to salvation only work for church folk. But for those whose starting point is far afield from most church membership requirements, and who have no cultural mooring in right-wrong rationales, a grace-centered explanation of the gospel is needed. For them, a rebuke of their lifestyle seems primitive and arrogant, while a simple invitation to walk with an understanding Savior is a welcomed thing.

Catholic priest and ecumenist Richard Rohr revealed that Jesus showed no interest in maintaining the purity systems of his day because they only appealed to religious ego and steered no one toward God.[10] Paul recognized this same cultural impasse two thousand years ago, and in a bold act he erased the right-wrong presentation of the gospel in favor of grace. If Paul would alter the path of salvation for the first-century Gentiles, why wouldn't we do the same for the seculars who live in our towns?

9

PROTECTING NEW VISION

"No one puts new wine into old wineskins. For the new wine would burst the wineskins, spilling the wine."
—Luke 5:37

A new vision is frail. For our church, finding a compelling vision turned out to be the easy part; protecting the vision was actually where leadership challenge became difficult. What surprised us was how many different enemies assembled to dismantle and dissolve our vision. Several of these enemies were well-meaning Christians who felt they were to save us from certain disaster. Thankfully, the Lord kept a flood of information flowing our way from great missiological leaders. Their voices encouraged us to persevere in our new calling and protect this vision as if it were a precious child that had been placed in our hands by the Lord himself. But there were twists and turns in this effort.

Unexpected Grief

In the wake of our early successes came a surprising wave
of grief. While we processed why we were feeling teary in
the day of harvest, it dawned on us that by saying yes to
the dinner church call, we were simultaneously saying no
to our old cherished dream, the Sunday-morning experience. This became felt when we moved from our church
campus to a community center so we could do a second,
brunch gathering for those neighbors. It was a huge
neighborhood and a great opportunity for the gospel, but
there was grief. Then, when the brunch church outgrew
the earlier, traditional gathering, it became obvious that
Seattle desired the dinner template over the proclamation template, and that led to more grief.

It became clear that we would never again enjoy the
sacred feeling of our sanctuary, the music, the prayer,
the lighting, the old rugged cross that was up front,
and the place where we had experienced many meaningful times with the Lord. What was replacing the
cherished vision were hard plastic chairs, temporary
speakers, harsh sound echoes that drove our musicians
out of their minds, and an entire hour of worship that
competed with basketball league whistles, loud laughter
in the halls, and all sounds that accompany a community center. While we were gaining the attention of a lot
of people for Christ, it was at the cost of our traditional
worship experience. By saying yes to the lost people of
our city, we were saying no to our saints.

The grief started initially with the leaders before
the move out of our building, but it began to fill the
hearts of our people immediately following. This
wave of grief was actually the first threat to the new
vision. We lost many attenders at this point who had

worshipped with us for years but simply did not want to give up the sacred feeling. The loss of friends combined with the loss of the cherished Sunday-morning experience caused our group to wrestle with the question, Is this really what Jesus wants us to do? Thankfully, our leaders were mature, and valued the need for grief. This was not a time to prove that we had heard God; it was a time to acknowledge the loss of the cherished dream, and give each other permission to grieve.

I remember well the Sunday morning when I stood and told everyone how much Melodee and I had been grieving the loss of our sacred Sunday experience. Along with the rest of the leaders, I invited the church into a season of grief, because we were giving up a lot to leave our sanctuary space behind and host dinner churches throughout our city.

In looking back, if we hadn't taken time to embrace the loss, we wouldn't have been available in heart for the dinner church call. This is why Jesus said, "Count the cost" (Luke 14:28), because without taking time to measure the sacrifice, it would eat away at the foundation of our commitment to the Lord's new future for us. Just as the vision of the Promised Land was first threatened by the Israelites longing for the leeks and garlics of Egypt, so our dinner church vision was threatened by our sense of loss. But after the season of grief came a season of "Let's do this." The dinner church vision had survived; the new wine was preserved.

A Soft Touch and a Slow Pace

A vision has to be unfolded in such a way that people's hearts have time to form around it. There is a leadership idea that every church has a set of values that you must work with when finding new vision. I would propose that exactly the opposite is closer to the reality. Every vision requires a certain set of values that are emotionally held by the people to accomplish it. Accordingly, values must be given time to reshape around a new vision, or else the "want to" to fulfill the vision will never form. Thus, the question isn't, What are our values? as much as, What values does our call require? Once we realized that we were learning not only a new vision, but also a new set of values to emotionally sustain the new vision, it was obvious that a soft touch and a slow pace were what our group needed.

There is an interesting account in the Old Testament about Solomon's son, Rehoboam. He was young and brash as he took his father's place on the throne, and he wanted to make sweeping changes in the kingdom. The leaders came to him and asked him to reduce the pressure his father had imposed, and if he would, they would be loyal to his leadership (2 Chronicles 10:4). Rehoboam decided to follow his young advisers' advice to declare that his little finger would be thicker than his father's waist, and that he would impose heavier burdens on them (vv. 9–14). He split the kingdom that day. His lack of appreciation for a soft touch and a slow pace of change cost him more than he ever expected, and his vision for the kingdom was never realized. In Jesus' words, the new wine (Rehoboam) burst the old wineskins (the kingdom), and both were ruined.

It is said there are three different ways to bring change: revolution, subversion, or by telling an alternate story. Revolution is fast and forceful, as was Rehoboam's choice. Subversion is slow because it eats away at the status quo, but it has in inherent risk that another vision, just as unfavorable as the one being subverted, will arise in the void. Subversion-change strategies spend their energies tearing down existing structures without having an opportunity to craft a replacement vision. Our founder, Christ himself, chose the third option and told an alternate story of the inbreaking kingdom of God. His parables and vision phrases stand as the greatest example in all of human history of the power of the alternate story to bring change.

Further, because our Master chose this form of change making, we as his followers are limited to the same, unless we have no interest in Christlikeness. This is a serious point for Christian leaders to meditate upon. Your personality might lean toward forcefulness, like Rehoboam, but Christ chose the alternate-story approach to change. Your personality might lean toward subversive approaches, but our Lord already chose the approach to change that he wants to empower his gospel: tell a different story. And that choice only works with a soft touch and a slow pace. Paul understood the importance of soft and slow, and told Timothy to be patient as a spiritual leader, even with difficult people (2 Timothy 2:24–25). This leadership discipline is critical to bringing about a new vision.

One Drop at a Time

The metaphor of the tipping point has become widely used to inform wise leadership during transitions, both in the business world and the church world. While different consultants have explained the tipping point principle in different ways, our leadership team envisioned it as a teeter-totter with a bucket on each end. The bucket on the left represented the old, cherished ways, and it was full; the bucket on the right represented the new vision, and it was empty. The role of the leaders during a transitional season was to put substance into the new-vision bucket, while allowing evaporation in the form of inattention to decrease the substance in the old, cherished-ways bucket. This required patience, because the filling of the new-vision bucket occurred one drop at a time. By verbalizing one story, one vision phrase, one comment day after day, the new bucket starts to fill. But the group is not ready to invest their heart and soul into the new vision until the day the tipping point is reached. The tipping point occurs when the new-vision bucket becomes one drop fuller than the old, cherished-way bucket, and the teeter-totter shifts on its axis, signaling that the most influential part of their story is now the new vision.

We saw this tipping point principle work exactly as predicted in our season of transition. We talked about dinner church, told stories about dinner church wins, read scripture after scripture about the ancient dinner churches, and showed pictures of dinner churches in action, day after day, week after week, until one day it became obvious that our church really wanted to take Seattle neighborhoods to heaven. And in a very short span of months, the identity of our church went from a traditional family church to a dinner church, with the rescue of Seattle souls on our minds. The tipping point had occurred.

Social Constructs

Jesus told a parable about wine and wineskins (Luke 5:37–39). He used this metaphor to protect the vision he was sent to launch—the new kingdom of God. I have heard many Christians over the years use this story to warn young leaders to not break the wineskins, but that was not Jesus' point. While this might seem like a contrast to the previous section, saving the wineskins was not the key point. Protecting the new wine was his point. The worst outcome for Jesus was not that the wineskins might break; it was that the beautiful new wine might be spilled all over the floor and lost forever. How many beautiful visions has the Lord sent to his leaders, only to have them be spilled all over the ground of church politics? How many churches are languishing in decline while one new vision after another is being spilled all over their boardrooms and congregational meetings? This is tragic.

Jesus' largest point in this parable, however, was the secret he gave to establishing new vision. The secret is in the imagery of the wineskin itself. What is a wineskin? It is a social construct that houses a vision; in ecclesial terms, it is a church family that houses a particular calling. According to Jesus, new vision must be housed in a new social construct. This point is so obvious, and yet it is seldom discussed in leadership vision-planning sessions.

Leaders after leaders are casting wonderful new visions across the land, but they are not changing the social construct of their churches to house it. Thus, the old social construct flexes against the new vision, the people react, the unity of the group breaks, the new vision is poured out all over the leadership meeting, and the pastor retreats to the safety of his office, frustrated with his people. I know this pattern because I have experienced it—more than once.

Most of the new vision that is being delivered into Christian communities today will never thrive in the proclamation template of church. What they need is a different template, a different place, a different time, and a different kind of personnel to help launch it. Let me say it again: every vision has to have an appropriate social construct to house it, and existing church constructs are probably never going to enable a new vision to thrive; they were never built for that new vision.

Once we heard the call to do church for the seculars, the poor, and the lonely who lived in sore Seattle neighborhoods, we knew our way of doing church was over. If our sacred Sunday-morning proclamation events had any resonance with that group at all, they would already be coming to us. Our decline year after year was proof positive that our way of doing church had no future. When we finally stumbled into the dinner church theology, we saw it as the perfect social construct to house the vision of taking sore urban neighborhoods to heaven. We now had a vision with an appropriate social construct to house it that would not spill the new wine the Lord was delivering to us.

Protecting against the Status Quo

The status quo is a powerful thing. Once people memorize a particular way of doing things, they put themselves on autopilot and just keep doing it without question. The momentum of the status quo is like a freight train that rolls along, and any leader who feels led to introduce a turn will more likely get mowed down than succeed.

Back at the very beginning of our change process, I called a meeting to introduce the idea that we needed to change some things if we were going to matter to Seattle. There were about sixty men present, and I played a short clip from the movie *Other People's Money*. In this clip, the owner of a cable company was telling a large room full of employees why the company was going to recover, though it had lost money for the past couple of years. It was inspiring to hear the old man cheerlead his troops.

When he was done, the character played by Danny DeVito walked up to the stage and started applauding the old man's speech and told the room that nobody in America cares about their cable anymore and are not going to buy it. He then reached into his pocket and pulled out a three-inch piece of cable and explained that it was a fiber-optics cable that could carry a hundred times more information than their outdated cable. He ended his object lesson by asking why anyone in the country would buy their cable when they could buy a fiber-optics cable and get one hundred times the calls?[1]

I stopped the clip and explained that our church was in a similar place. Our way of doing church only mattered to the already-saved, and we were slipping into irrelevance with our neighbors. I then asked them to help me prayerfully hear from the Lord how we could become more effective with our own neighbors. I don't know what I expected, but I could not have been more underwhelmed by their response. Every man in that room got up from his chair and left without saying a word to me. No one said, "Wow. That's interesting," or, "I'll be praying with you," or, "I'll think on this and shoot you an e-mail." Nothing! What happened that night was I got steamrolled by the momentum of the status quo. In their minds, their church had been around a long time, and it would continue to flourish just because it always had. Thus, my warning to them was completely ignored. That would be the first of many status quo steamrolling experiences I would encounter in that historic church.

Status quo is a powerful thing that can kill a new vision dead in just one meeting. Thankfully, eight years later that same group would cease their obsession with the status quo and respond to a new vision with a lion-like boldness. Status quo freight trains can be stopped, but until such time, leaders must throw themselves in front of those trains and be undeterred in their resolve to protect the vision the Lord is trying to impart into the future of that church.

Protecting against the Reformation Template

Another interesting pressure that attempted to dissolve our vision came when we started being discounted as a parachurch ministry. We realized there were Reformation blinders on many church leaders who came to visit our churches that disabled them from seeing them as full-fledged churches. We have lived in the Reformation era for more than five hundred years, and it has normalized a purity system and an organizational structure with certain metrics of spiritual development that are quite complex. This background causes many to misread the simple power of the dinner table theology. The Reformation era, which was designed to get people into the Scriptures and provide mile markers of disci-pleship, has created Christians that have no ability to see the spiritual-development capacity of the dinner church because it does not look like the ways they are developing Christians. Because the dinner churches do not fit their metrics, they have to rename what we are doing into something different.

We found that we have to clearly and bluntly state what a dinner church is *not* in order to confront their blindness. First, it is not an outreach; it is a church. Outreaches do not have everything necessary to spiritual development. Second, it is not a food program; it is a church. There are all kinds of food programs that keep people from starving to death. A dinner church uses food to reveal the gospel, but then it offers the gospel to the full. Third, it is not a Christian group doing nonprofit work; it is a church. As good as that is for churches to partner with nonprofits, that is not what this is. Fourth, it is not a ministry; it is a church. Ministries are an arm of a church, but cannot fully function in the purposes of a scriptural church. Fifth, it is not a parachurch group; it is a church.

In fact, the dinner church is far more present in Scripture than any other form of church that has ever been established. So, if Jesus and the apostles felt comfortable to call the dinner-centric gatherings church, then so should we. With these scripturally based arguments and more, we protect the vision.

Protecting Sinners from Saints

There are some pockets of the faith who believe it is their Christian responsibility to rebuke sinners, but most do not think that way. However, when saints insist on church approaches that please them, and support no vision that resonates with the lost, they are blocking the path to salvation. Similarly, when saints insist that church resources be spent on their favorite programs, leaving no funds for lifting the poor or reaching the unsaved, they are blocking the path of salvation and impeding the rescue mission of the church. These entitled attitudes create a situation in which the needs of the lost must be protected from the wants of the saints.

It is surprising how many leaders know they are supposed to rescue the lost but are not willing to talk to their saints about changing their way of doing church so the unsaved can join them. While I am deeply grateful for the heritage of the faith that has brought us all to this point, there is no value in allowing the last chapter of the church to destroy the new chapters of the church that are trying to form. The older saints usually don't openly attack newly forming chapters; they just starve them by withholding funds and encouragement.

While the American church spends its time obsessing over the proclamation template, the statistics continue to stack up that the lost are not joining our gatherings. The occasional prodigal does come running home, and that is awesome when it happens. But that is not the same thing as rescuing seculars. If the saints continue to have their way, and the proclamation template continues to be the obsession of the times, it is the sinners who will pay the price. The greatest reaction we feel when saints tried to ignore or starve fresh expressions of the church is to provide an energetic defense for the sinners. I invite you to join us in the defense of the lost. In so doing we are preserving the new wine—that beautiful, missional wine.

Protecting the Poor from the Rich

Most churches in America are planted in middle- and upper-class neighborhoods because that is the only population that can afford the expensive proclamation church. Accordingly, an unintended elitism has formed in many Christians that, frankly, is a perfect fit with suburban values. So, when many Christians and leaders see a dinner church, and they see the low-income nature of many of the guests, they start looking for kind ways to communicate how it was not their calling to work with the poor.

I would propose for all of us to consider that Jesus spent much of his time with sinners and with the poor. And if we are called to replicate his likeness here on earth, we might want to find ways to do the same. In defending the dinner church vision, we are protecting a way of church that the poor can sociologically relate to.

One of the hardest things for me is driving through other towns and seeing one sore neighborhood after another where a dinner church would thrive, and then seeing numerous proclamation churches just a few blocks away that are spending all of their influence on the already-saved. It just doesn't seem fair. I certainly talk about it every chance I get, hoping to motivate leaders to take responsibility for the hurting populace located near them. In some small way, I am defending the poor. And every once in a while, we win and actually inspire a leader to take a dinner church into an ignored neighborhood. We must defend the poor against church structures that are ignoring them. Jesus tipped over tables in the defense of the poor. We are on good ground to mount a defense of our own.

Protecting the Young from the Old

One age group that is becoming increasingly absent from the church in America is the millennials. While there are many reasons for this, it is clear that the traditional church is not resonating with the young. The young people who have tried to talk to church leadership about considering the perspectives of their age group have all too often walked away feeling ignored. In fairness to church leaders, it is not an easy nut to crack. Millennials are called the *compassion generation*, which means that social-lift initiatives for marginalized people speak to millennials' Christianity. But many churches are hierarchal organizations, and church structures look more like big business than what millennials can stomach.

We have been amazed by the large numbers of people in their twenties and thirties who are looking for a church that is more about serving than talking. While this is not to pat ourselves on the back, it reveals an interest and a potential reengagement point for the millennials that is worthy of consideration for all church leaders. Almost all of our dinner churches have a core of millennials that have adopted us as their church and are the backbone of our serving ethos. It is amazing to see a long line of broken people being served by a long line of young adults, and then see those millennials sit at the tables and breathe life into lonely middle- and upper-aged adults. It is a picture of the grandkids lifting the grandparents of society. Protecting new wine might be protecting the heartbeat of the young and that beautiful value of compassion.

Protecting the Verb Church from the Noun Church

Our churches have become so developed over the decades that an organizational identity has formed in each group. Rather than churches being the collective works of its individual Christians, they have become a thing (a noun). Due to brand building and marketing, most churches have published their unique identity to be considered against other churches in the area: "them" (a pronoun). That contrasts sharply with the church in the apostolic era who saw themselves as expressing the works of Christ together (a verb).

Our group realized that if we were ever going to say yes to the Lord in reaching the sinners, the broken, and the seculars of our city, we would need to take our historic talking church, and shift to a serving church. We would have to move from being a noun to being a verb. We also needed to cease focusing our efforts on teaching and focus them, instead, on serving table churches to people who really needed the help.

To honor the decision to become a verb church, we changed our name from Westminster Community Church to Community Dinners, which is what we were being called on the streets. We could make sense to Christians by choosing a name that focused on *being*, or we could make sense to the people on the sidewalk choosing a name that emphasized *doing*. We selected the name that better spoke to what we were *doing*: serving Jesus dinners. The Christian community still stumbles on our name, but we aren't called to reach them. We are called to the strangers, sinners, broken, poor, and lonely people that fill our city.

A world theological movement was started by the Lausanne Congress in 1974. While America has been largely absent from this gathering of world Christian leaders, these leaders have collectively formed a statement to help correct the obsession of the proclamation-based approach to church. The statement that inspired the movement was: "Never again shall the gospel be conceived as proclamation only, but proclamation with social engagement in equal measure."[2] In other words, the Christian church around the world realized the empty results of a church approach that only talked about the gospel. This was especially shallow when contrasted with the Scriptures, which inspire the church to engage in the social needs of its day, but do so in a way where the gospel can be proclaimed.

Some groups have grabbed hold of this to some degree and added a bevy of service opportunities to their ministries. While that is better than doing nothing, the poor and the lost are not finding their way into the gatherings that merely talk about Christ. While those churches are doing both proclamation and social engagement, they are not engaging in a way that offers the proclaimed gospel and the served gospel in the same setting.

This makes the dinner church a beautiful option, because there the poor and the lost receive both the served gospel and the proclaimed gospel in the same room, and at the same time. This is probably why Jesus embedded the gospel into the dinner table construct at the Last Supper.

10

SORE NEIGHBORHOODS

> *"Healthy people don't need a doctor—*
> *sick people do. I have come to call not*
> *those who think they are righteous, but*
> *those who know they are sinners."*
>
> —Mark 2:17

For eighty-five years our church served suburban families on the edge of the city. One day it dawned on us that there were very few families left in our neighborhood. Further, most of the families who attended our church drove in from suburban neighborhoods located even farther away from the center of Seattle than the church campus was. We were forced to learn about "neighborhood theology" in a trial-by-fire manner. In other words, we had to learn it well and learn it fast, or we were going to die.

Pastor and church leadership consultant Alan Roxburgh has noted that almost all of the stories in the New Testament occurred in a neighborhood.[1] Neighborhood theology is being talked about more and more in seminaries. Sometimes it is referred to as the "theology of place," and other times "the parish model," but they all speak the same language. Neighborhood theology can be defined as the intentional effort of going back to the parish model of church, which was the predominant vision before the church-growth movement. It can also be defined as the church's return to the neighborhood, in which a group exists to know and serve the greatest needs of its immediate neighbors.

We found ourselves guilty of inwardness in our Seattle story, and had no understanding of the theology of neighborhood. When we followed the Lord to a new way of functioning, we saw Jesus doing a great many things in Seattle neighborhoods. And as he waved for us to join him, we started to see one sore neighborhood after another. It both broke our hearts and called us out of our inwardness. A neighborhood theology came alive in us.

All Places Are Not the Same

The church-growth movement of the 1960s brought many positive insights to the American landscape. However, one negative result is that it focused leaders so intently on their organization and strategies that it blinded them to the importance of place. Further, it created such a common vision of church that leaders actually began to believe that if they organized their churches according to the church-growth metrics, they would thrive no matter where they were located. These ideas eclipsed the theology of place almost altogether.

But not all places are the same. If a church is located in suburbia, where families are the predominant social circle, then church-growth ideas work quite well when done right. However, if a church is located in an urban neighborhood in which singles are the predominant social circle, or in an impoverished neighborhood in which the lower third are the predominant social circle, then church-growth ideas will likely fail. This is why so many churches have moved out of our cities; they haven't known how to do anything but the proclamation template, so they shrank into irrelevance, and then faced the choice to close down or move out.

The theology of place gets leaders refocused on the social circles that exist in a particular area of their calling, and informs what kind of church resonates with the people who live there. For us, our calling directed us into sore urban neighborhoods that had significant populations of the marginalized and lonely. And with the proclamation template statistically being ineffective with that social circle, we needed to change, even though the proclamation church was all we knew.

Who Jesus Sought

Christian leaders fall into two camps: (1) those who target no one, claiming the gospel is for "whosoever will," and (2) those who target a particular demographic of people in their city that they want to reach. Surprisingly, Jesus did not use either of those approaches. He targeted a particular kind of person, not on the basis of demographics, but rather on the narrower basis of socio-economics. Jesus was far more interested in those who had great need than all others who did not. While this is scripturally provable in countless locations, one of my favorite verses is when Jesus spoke of coming for people who knew they needed a physician, and not the healthy ones (Mark 2:17). How interesting.

Most churches are killing themselves to attract people into their building that do not feel much of a need for help. I have often wondered how different the American church would be if we simply reached out for those who already know that they need help, instead of competing for those who may not feel that need right now.

The day Jesus went to the synagogue and read from the scroll of Isaiah was his version of publishing a mission statement. He read:

> The Spirit of the LORD is upon me, for he has anointed me to bring Good News to the poor. He has sent me to proclaim that captives will be released, that the blind will see, that the oppressed will be set free, and that the time of the LORD's favor has come. (Luke 4:18–19)

The wording Jesus repeated the most from that mission statement was "Good News to the poor." He used those words again when John the Baptist sent his disciples to ask Jesus if he was really the Messiah. Jesus told them to go back and tell John that the "Good News [gospel] is being preached to the poor" (Luke 7:22). That phraseology was Jesus' proof of his Messianic identity. Christ's rescue mission was indelibly welded to the poor.

Jesus' parable about the sheep and the goats in Matthew 25 speaks of a day when a serious separation between people will occur on the basis of one thing: how they responded to the poor. In Jesus' story, those who took care of the poor, the hungry, the widow, and the prisoner were likened to sheep and given favorable standing. However, those who overlooked the poor, the hungry, the widow, and the prisoner were likened to stubborn goats and given an unfavorable status. This should be a sobering story for the American church, especially when we have overlooked the poor in our efforts to fill our Sunday-morning gatherings with well-to-do people. In this way, the church has jumped the tracks that Christ laid down for us.

Native Territory for the Church

After the ascension of Christ, the church was officially in the apostles' hands. True to the example of Christ, the apostles gave the poor a preferential place in the newly forming church. In fact, Acts 6 records the first internal conflict, which was over better care for the poor widows. Think of it: a church fight over better care for the poor. In fact, the role of the deacon would not have emerged if the young church did not desire to provide better care for the poor. Perhaps there will come a day when the role of deacon will be won back from the boardroom to the all-important role of lifting the poor.

From that day forward, the apostolic era revealed one chapter after another where the fusion between the church and the poor became cemented. The agape feasts and the poor laundry workers were gossiping the gospel through the large cities of the Pax Romana. When the plagues decimated many Roman cities and killed 30 to 40 percent of their inhabitants, it was the Christians who stayed behind, without regard for their own welfare, and tended to the sick and nursed many of them back to health.[2] The church made a great mark on the Roman world because of their willingness to prefer the poor and the sick. "When Constantine declared Rome the Holy Roman Empire, it wasn't for political reasons, as it was already Christianized, he just recognized the realities."[3]

Preference of the poor led to preference of the church. That is no small consideration.

Further demonstrations of the fusion of the church and the poor have been revealed through the centuries. The Franciscans, a monastic order, and the Poor Clares, monastic nuns, took vows of poverty so they would never find themselves uncomfortable to be with the poor. Further, they both developed numerous ways to support the impoverished populations. In sixteenth-century England, as much as 50 percent of the population faced grinding poverty and vagrancy.[4] This set the stage for the Stranger's Friend Society developed by John Wesley in the late 1700s, who dedicated themselves to ministry among London's urban poor.[5] Then, in the 1800s, William Booth's Salvation Army responded to London at a time when it had eighty thousand prostitutes, with a vision that everyone have at least the life of a cab horse—shelter at night, food to eat, and work to do.[6] These are just a few of the many examples of the church exercising the theology of poverty. Lifting the poor is native territory for the church of Jesus.

No Theology of Poverty

In the beginning of our dinner church movement, we did not have a good theology of poverty. Furthermore, we did not know there was such a thing. But as we found ourselves in the midst of sore Seattle neighborhoods, we sensed we were lacking the soul depth necessary to work with Jesus in this environment long term. Then the Scriptures began to speak to us in sobering and voluminous ways. There are twenty-three hundred verses in the Bible about the poor; it is a central message of Scripture, surpassed only by the theme of redemption.[7] Given this volume of scriptural content focused on the poor, it is interesting how the American church has held it as a minor theology. Giving preferential place to the poor is anything but a minor theology.

"You will always have the poor among you" (Mark 14:7). Jesus uttered those words in three of the four Gospels in defense of a woman's expensive worship. However, there is a deeper assumption in these words. Most Christians read this verse as a prediction, when it is actually stating a necessity. The church needs the poor as much as the poor needs the church. The poor provide for our greatest worship; when we are adoring the poor, we are actually adoring Christ. The poor also provide for our greatest discipleship; when we are responding to the poor, we are practicing the works of Christ. The poor also provide for our greatest mission; when we are lifting the poor, we are entering society through a door where we will be welcomed. The poor are not just a fact of life; they are the intended intersection for the Savior to enter the affairs of this world. That is why Jesus often repeated the refrain that he was bringing the good news (gospel) to the poor. That was both the identifier of his Savior role and the method of his rescue plan on earth. This, arguably, serves as the cornerstone for the rich theology of poverty.

Life in the Lower Third

In wealthy America we have overlooked the need for a theology of poverty, assuming that everyone here is middle-class and well-fed. That assumption is not true, and never was. In 2012, two out of five American families visited a food bank.[8] The 2010 Census revealed that some American cities had 29 percent of their population living beneath the poverty line.[9] Philip Yancey, editor at large for *Christianity Today* magazine, reported that one-third of all dog and cat food was purchased by senior citizens too poor to afford human food.[10] This is no longer middle-class America; things are changing.

Most church leaders believe that America is primarily filled with middle- and upper-class people and, thus, they plan their churches for that population. However, the lower class has always existed, that third of the population that earns below middle-class incomes. Statistically, one out of every three neighborhoods is populated by the lower third in every town across the country, so it makes for dishonest missiologists to pretend they are not among us. While these populations commonly avoid the main streets, they are still a part of our towns.

Church leaders are often blind to these populations because they do not attend our Sunday gatherings, and probably never will. Our weekend proclamation gatherings do not match their sociological realities; not only do they feel embarrassed to gather with the well-dressed people who fill most of our churches; they also find it difficult to sit through a Sunday-morning service, where they must sing a number of songs and then listen to a forty-minute sermon, when they are filled with anxiety about what their children will eat that night and how they will make rent the next day. Those are the realities of life in the lower third.

Unintended Elitism

An honest review of the past one hundred years reveals that almost all churches have been located in middle- and upper-class neighborhoods because that is where the people live who can afford our expensive way of doing church. Church campuses and large staff salaries have made the proclamation model a very expensive endeavor; a savvy church leader knows that only upper-tier people can pay for such an approach. This has created an unintended elitism. We never set out to ignore the poor, but our need to balance our large budgets has made elitists of us nonetheless.

While we have told ourselves that we welcome the poor in our midst, they have not come. Some groups engage in outreaches to the poor, but still the poor have not joined the worship gatherings. As stated earlier, our proclamation churches do not fit the sociology of the poor. A fisherman may say he fishes for halibut, but if he uses a worm and fishes on a lake, he's fishing for trout. Words do not determine which fish is caught; the bait and the strategy do. Similarly, welcoming words do not determine if the poor will join us; our way of doing church does.

There is an interesting correlation between the present-day church and the story of Jesus cleansing the temple. The very day Jesus entered into Jerusalem on the donkey, he went to the temple and tipped over the tables of the money changers who were selling sacrificial doves for exorbitant prices, and chased them off. But it was what happened in the next verse that is most compelling. The blind and the lame came to the very porch where the money changers had been, and Jesus healed them (Matthew 21:12–14). Somehow, the place in which heaven and earth were supposed to meet had been co-opted by greed, and the poor who could not afford the overpriced sacrifices had been quietly displaced. It seems that no one even noticed their absence until the day Jesus made a public issue of it.

Does the average church notice their absence? Middle- and upper-class churches today find themselves in a similar place. We have built buildings and created structures that assume everyone can engage, but the poor are not present. Our way of doing church just doesn't match their realities. Someone from the lower third does not walk into the nice boutiques on Main Street for the same reason he or she does not walk into our nice buildings with our nicely dressed people either. Yet many church leaders barely notice that the lower third are not worshipping with us and, worse yet, may even breathe a sigh of relief that they are not in attendance, so as not to have to deal with congregational complaints. While not all traditional churches have overlooked the poor, most have, and find themselves not too dissimilar from the elitism of the temple in Jesus' day.

Neighborhood Theology

Any church that looks to recover its sense of mission, or any new church that looks to establish its mission, will find it difficult if it does not have a neighborhood theology. For most of my pastoral ministry, I functioned without a neighborhood theology and found the leadership ideas of mission and vision incredibly difficult to capture in a clear way. This was because I was trying to figure out our church's mission and vision, rather than behold the social circle I was supposed to rescue. In other words, I felt I was supposed to create a "this is who we are" statement rather than a "this is who they are" rescue response. This was the natural result of an inadequate neighborhood theology. But in the midst of our season of decline, the Lord directed us back into a specific neighborhood with a specific people. This changed everything.

Before the automobile, the parish churches in America resembled a neighborhood theology. They were located in the center of a town where they were easy to get to. While they still had a proclamation-centered assumption, they also had a neighborhood identity. However, after the automobile expanded people's ability to enlarge their circle of living, neighborhood identity began to dwindle, and this affected the assumption of whom the church was now serving. The neighborhood circle widened to a region, or an area. Further, when the church-growth movement directed leaders to focus on the quality of ministry they were offering, leaders were redirected from serving the neighborhood to attracting the wider region. This subtle shift changed the question leaders were answering from, What does our neighborhood need? to, Who are we?

A neighborhood focus directs leaders to respond to the needs of that neighborhood; a regional focus is too broad to respond to a particular social circle or particular set of needs. So, they are forced by sheer scale to create a ministry expression around who they are and what they do. The church-growth movement became so pervasive in most denominations that even smaller neighborhood churches felt compelled to create the statements of "this is who we are," and develop subsequent brand building to the point that they lost what they were great at: neighborhood response. In these ways, the neighborhood theology became eclipsed in most of our churches.

But this idea of neighborhood theology needs to be drilled down to a deeper level to fully understand it. Mission strategist Alan Hirsch believes that one of the original apostolic ideas that has fallen on hard times in recent eras has been identifying and entering into under-gospeled social circles.[11] This was seen first in Jerusalem, where the detractors of the gospel complained that the first church had filled the entire city with its teaching (Acts 5:28). And how did they do it? By spreading from one social circle to the next. This is also visible in early church history in the way the believers spread through the large Hellenistic cities with such fullness that Christianity became synonymous with urban cities. These early-century Christians captured the attention of these large cities by spreading their house churches and feast churches from one under-gospeled social circle to the next in an intentional and continuous way. Theirs was a neighborhood theology.

Neighborhood theology is more than a church that does worship gatherings in a defined neighborhood. It is the collective family of Christ-followers who hear a calling to enter into an under-gospeled social circle within their neighborhood and do church for them—whatever that means. This is the essence of the neighborhood theology. Eric Jacobsen, senior pastor of Tacoma's First Presbyterian Church, uses the question, "What is God doing in the neighborhood?" to get his church thinking outside of its internal programs.[12] That is a great question for every group to ask because it positions them to hear a calling into a particular social circle. Their response to that calling will enable them to create a healthy neighborhood theology.

In our church story, once we felt called to a particular neighborhood, we began to observe a social circle in that neighborhood. And when we focused on who they were, the dinner church vision made perfect sense; it was a perfect fit. While it was not our favorite way of doing church, it was a way that would matter to them. Often, I have other church leaders tell me how easy it is to understand our mission and vision. But that clarity of mission is a direct result of adopting a neighborhood theology, hearing a call into some particular social circles, and then offering a way of doing church that they need. Crafting mission and vision from the inside was a blurry and frustrating exercise for us. But crafting mission and vision by observing a particular social circle, that was far easier.

Spreading through the City

To narrow a leadership scope down to a neighborhood, and then narrow it even further to specific social circles, makes it easy to see the next under-gospeled social circles and how to do church for them too. Missionary Alan Johnson, who ministers in the slums of Bangkok, Thailand, stated that one of apostolic ideas in those early days of the church was "citywide-ness."[13] The social circles that the Lord gave us eyes to see in Seattle were: (1) the marginalized, which included the working poor; (2) the isolated, which included the second-life singles;

and (3) the Samaritans, humanitarians who were not necessarily Christ-followers. These three social circles had been largely overlooked by churches, and yet were profoundly present in neighborhood after neighborhood throughout our city.

That observation created an immediate question: If we can serve these social circles in one neighborhood, why not spread to another neighborhood and take those people to heaven too? We had already learned that the church-around-the-dinner-table template resonated with these three social circles, and we weren't doing anything on other weeknights anyway, so we let another neighborhood adopt us. And we found the same divine spark that we found in the first neighborhood. Before long the question surfaced again: If we can do this in two neighborhoods, why not another? Without realizing it, we were inching our way toward the apostolic practice of citywide-ness. Now we own the citywide theology straight up and without apology, and are setting our sights to have a dinner church in twenty-seven sore neighborhoods throughout the city.

In 2015, we were featured in a local television and radio news cycle. One of the items the reporters decided to feature was how many dinner churches were now functioning in Seattle. One of the radio hosts even said that if he were to ever start going to church, he would rather do it around a table. We were shocked by the positive tone of the press in such a secular environment. This was one of many indicators of how the dinner table template fits the secular population, and to not spread through the city would be a tragedy for the lost, lonely, and seculars that live in our sore neighborhoods. Perhaps one day it will be said of us as it was said of the

Jerusalem church, "You have filled [your city] with your teaching about [Jesus]" (Acts 5:28).

An Eye for Sore Places

When we saw the divine spark occur among the unsaved in our Jesus dinners, we were grateful to finally have some traction in the urban setting. The church has been waning in our big cities, and is now down to a pitifully low church-to-population ratio. So, any effectiveness experienced there was a big deal to us. Initially, we thought the dinner church was an urban thing—God's way of getting the church back into the big cities. That is, until a small town near us called and asked for insight so they could start a dinner church in their town.

While I did not try to talk them out of it, I did offer a disclaimer that this was probably an urban church approach, but the disclaimer must not have been very effective because they were not dissuaded. They started their dinner church in the same way we had started ours, and within a year were running almost as many as we had in some of our urban neighborhoods. I still remember the day their pastor called me to say he had just baptized four people who had come to Christ at their dinner church. I hung up the phone and officially reversed my position that this was an urban movement.

I have since concluded that the dinner church will resonate in any neighborhood in which soreness exists; whether in urban centers, midsized cities, or rural townships. If there are neighborhoods with the marginalized, the working poor, or the lonely populations, there will be an interested response to a weeknight dinner church—the kind of response that church leaders seldom see.

It is a great day in the life of a pastor or a church planter when he or she starts to see how many people in that town live below the middle-class income levels, and then acknowledge that these large groups are absent from the traditional churches that are gathering nearby. Further, when a leader develops an eye for the sore neighborhoods that the lower third inhabits, he or she will behold a profound opportunity for church planting. The day of planters choosing their sites based on where they want to raise their kids is waning, and the day of planters choosing their sites based on sore-ness is coming. I propose that the greatest missiological opportunity for church planting, especially for the dinner church, is America's sore neighborhoods. And there are thousands of them with no church presence.

Every Church with a Dinner Church

Church planting has taken on several different forms in the past couple of decades. It used to be that a church planter would assemble a team and start a church from scratch. Today, various kinds of partnerships are forming between existing churches and planters in start-up efforts. This is often due to the need for planters to have partners with deep pockets to sustain them for a season. The fact that only 50 percent of church plants survive to see their first birthday for financial reasons hovers in every planter's mind.[14]

The effectiveness of the dinner church, however, opens up a different way of church planting—something existing groups can initiate. Dinner churches function any night of the week, so established groups that have musicians, cooks, preachers, and volunteers can now cook up a feast on a weeknight, take it to a community space in a nearby sore neighborhood, and open up a dinner church of their own as a second church. Most churches are sophisticated enough to do a proclamation church on Sundays, and then do a dinner church on a weeknight. When an existing church plants a dinner church, it is very inexpensive and is affordable for even small groups to plant. And what better way for a church to expand their influence than to walk into a nearby sore neighborhood with a Jesus dinner in their hands and a Jesus story on their lips? The church in America would change our nation neighborhood by neighborhood if we adopted the idea of each church planting their own dinner church.

THE THING ABOUT MONEY

Jesus said, ". . . you feed them." "But we have only five loaves and two fish!" they answered. . . . Then he told the people to sit down on the grass. Jesus took the five loaves and two fish . . . and blessed them. . . . he gave the bread to the disciples, who distributed it to the people. They all ate as much as they wanted, and afterward, the disciples picked up twelve baskets of leftovers.
—Matthew 14:16–17, 19–20

Money is a big concern for leaders who are attempting to establish new churches. Of the large number of new churches that don't survive, it is usually not because of missional failure as much as because of running out of money before they attract enough tithers to support their efforts. A completely different attitude about money needs to form among our apostles, evangelists, and everyone who is working to extend the kingdom to new locations.

Twenty-seven years of visionary ministry had taught me a thing or two about financial decisions, GAAP

(Generally Accepted Accounting Principles), P&Ls (profit and loss statements), balance sheets, cash flow reports, loans, budgets, capital campaigns, bridge funding, and typical financial maturing seasons when launching a new vision. However, when we shifted from a proclamation church to a dinner church, my financial assumptions proved to be inadequate—*woefully* inadequate. It wasn't that I needed to learn more about finances; I somehow needed to learn less.

Jesus Dinners Are Different

There are a couple of Gospel accounts regarding resources that inspired a different attitude about money in our leadership team. They were the twin stories of the feeding of the five thousand (Matthew 14:16–21), and the feeding of the four thousand (Mark 8:4–9). In these we saw a pattern of how Jesus dinners work: (1) take the provision you have, even if it is only five loaves and two fish; (2) call everyone for dinner; and (3) the rest will show up unexplainably as you are getting the people seated. That's it. That is how Jesus dinners work. We began to see a strange similarity between this multiplication story and how our finances were beginning to work. It was both beautiful and frustrating. It was beautiful because we were now a part of a divine flow, but it was frustrating because the human calculator no longer explained all that was happening in our finances.

Our vast experience in budget making seemed to be futile. For instance, all of our efforts to fully fund our dinner churches on the front side dissolved away one after another; yet we never missed serving a meal. So, we had very little money when we opened our first dinner, and we have very little money now that we have seven dinner churches per week; and yet we have never missed a meal. In comparing notes with other leaders who do meals for the poor, there is a shared reality: we all feel as though we are two days from going out of business; yet we have never missed a meal. And that has been going on for decades for some groups across the country; it has been going on for almost one decade for us. But that is how the Jesus dinner works; it uses a God calculator. At times this calculator seems more like Jack Sparrow's compass than something you'd plug into the wall, but then again, it's a Jesus dinner. Let me hasten to say that we still use the human calculator as smartly as we know how, but it just doesn't explain as much as it used to. We have had to learn to rely on the God calculator too.

At the beginning of our dinner church journey, we assumed we would be going after grants and pursuing social agencies to partner with us. After all, we were already serving a hot sit-down meal to hundreds of Seattle's poor. But the Lord had other plans. One night I had one of those stirrings deep in my soul as I was trying to fall asleep. In that half-awake, half-asleep moment, I sensed Jesus asking me, "Verlon, don't you think I might want to pay for the dinner for the people I am giving you?" I had to admit that hadn't crossed my mind. But then I remembered the first two Jesus dinners and how Jesus had said to his disciples, "you feed them" (Matt. 14:16). In that moment, I realized what it must've felt like to be a disciple witnessing those thousands being fed, because that similar message was now coming to me. Yes, Jesus told me he wanted to pay for it, but I knew that we were his closest hands to this story, so it was actually going to involve us just as it had involved those first disciples, and there would be unexplainable stuff happening. But, I said yes anyway, and we stopped reaching out for grants and funding partners.

Truthfully, I am still baffled by how his provision works. But it works. The Jesus dinner pattern plays over and over again in our story: we bring what we have in hand, and the rest shows up unexplainably while we are getting the people seated at the tables. Go figure.

Tithe into Poverty

The Lord has historically paid his bills on earth by inspiring his followers to engage in tithing. But once he called us to rescue the marginalized and the isolated, new scriptures about the tithe began to emerge, verses we did not know were in the Bible. The origins of the tithe date back to the book of Deuteronomy and include the tithe into poverty, which was a third of all tithing (14:28–29). The tithe was God's age-old plan to lift the poor. So, we started challenging our people to tithe into poverty, and we quickly won back that scriptural form. That growth of understanding changed us and welded our hearts even closer to the poor whom we were befriending. After all, where our money is, there are our hearts also (Luke 12:34). In fact, the promises of God regarding those who give to the poor are significantly higher than for those who simply tithe. That was interesting.

Then another verse that we had never seen raised up like a clarion word from the Lord and changed our attitudes about money yet again. It says, in essence, that anyone who gives to the poor is actually lending

to the Lord, and he will repay (Proverbs 19:17). From
that verse we realized that because we were directing
our finances toward our dinner churches, which were
lifting large numbers of poor people, we were actually entering into a lender relationship with God, in
which we should expect repayment. Winning back this
theology really changed us. This is a different thing
than expecting blessings because we have tithed; it
was an actual lender relationship in which Jesus was
asking us for a loan to fund his dinners, and then he
would repay us. If this idea were not so clearly stated
in Scripture, I would think we were going off the rails;
it took some getting used to. But we ultimately took
the lender relationship as something that was his idea
and was a real offer to us, and entered into a formal
lending relationship with Christ. In these ways, God
reshaped our attitudes to function with the Jesus
dinner calculator.

Many senior leaders are noting that millennials
are struggling to tithe; in fact, they are just not doing
it. My sense is that big buildings, big salaries, big
budgets, and churches that run like big business are
frustrating our twenty-year-olds, and they don't want
to support that.

The millennials are becoming referred to more and
more as the "compassion generation" because of their
significant involvement in non-profits. After observing
the twentysomethings respond to our compassion-rich
dinner tables, we would agree that they are aptly named.
Millennials started finding our dinner gatherings and
started flowing into our leadership teams without invitation, or without us doing anything to seek them. They
just found us. The opportunity to serve the gospel,

befriend the stranger, lift the poor, and then proclaim the gospel really seemed to resonate with them. Some indicated that they were raised in a Christian home but had no desire to attend a Sunday church. However, the dinner church was now their home church.

The fact that these twenty-year-olds sought out our compassion-based church is a significant signal for church leaders to meditate on, especially in the light of their absence in most traditional churches across all denominational lines. I have a strong sense that the idea of tithing will surge among millennials if it is the *tithe into poverty* that is presented.

The Jesus Potluck

One of the practices of the early dinner churches was that the food was provided by the Christians as a potluck—a Jesus potluck, if you will. The Christ-followers brought larger portions of food than what their families needed, so as to create an overflow of food to feed the strangers, the sinners, and the poor who were invited in to share the evening with them. The potluck is seen most clearly in Scripture in the communion passage where Paul was disgusted with the Corinthian church because they were hoarding the food for themselves while leaving the poor standing aside (1 Corinthians 11:20–22). Though this verse was a rebuke that was designed to reorient the church as to how Christ wants his body to function for the poor, it reveals the potluck nature of the agape feasts. While our Seattle dinners are serving far too many people to do as a potluck, I am proposing the idea for existing churches to consider. It is inexpensive, it is easy in terms of preparation, and it is a rewarding way for a church to bring lift to a sore neighborhood in the name of Christ. While this would undoubtedly work best for churches that have many stay-at-home parents in their congregation, it can work for church-plant teams too. We have one dinner church that is small, and the plant team cooks all the food in their individual apartments, and then they bring it to their dinner gathering. They just consider it a part of their leadership function, and it doesn't take a ton of organization to accomplish. I am predicting that many more Jesus potlucks will be springing up across the land soon. It is too much of a Jesus idea to ignore.

Bi-Vocational Pastor

The assumption of pastors being fully supported did not come to be until the fourth century, when the government of Rome authorized Christianity as the state church. While there were periods during the apostolic era when it appears some of the church leaders were able to focus exclusively on church work, it was not the ruling assumption. It was more common for leaders to support themselves in different ways than church offerings. Paul sewed tents with Aquila and Pricilla's trading company, and they traveled throughout several of the large Hellenistic cities in their business. Paul traveled with them, worked with them, and planted the gospel in these cities as he went. Make no mistake about it; Paul was a bi-vocational church planter.

Now the church finds itself woefully behind in church planting. For all of our talk about church planting in recent decades, we are actually only opening as many churches per capita as during the two lowest points in American history: the Civil War and the Great Depression.[1] The American church will need to double-time and triple-time our church-planting rates to catch up to the church-to-population ratio we held before the church-growth movement.

This level of church planting necessitates a different assumption of funding for leadership. Throughout church history, whenever the church has been in a steep church-planting season, bi-vocational leadership has become the order of the day. This season of church planting will be no different. Once our leadership team felt the call to spread through the city with our dinner church plants, we realized that the bi-vocational approach to ministry was upon us. We pay our pastors for one day a week, and it is assumed that they will pastor their neighborhoods during the day and lead their dinner churches that night. The rest of the time, they are released to find employment to support their families. An effort is made to find jobs in the same neighborhoods they are called to pastor, for incarnational reasons.

Not only does the bi-vocational financial form make for a more affordable start-up budget; it makes for an incarnational manner of pastoral life—doing daily life with the very people one is called to reach. Many rich spiritual moments have developed in coffee shops and sidewalk conversations because our pastors were simply there. Melodee and I led the way, and were the first to move into the neighborhood we were planting. We spent countless hours in that six-block neighborhood. I still have pastoral conversations on the sidewalks in that neighborhood, even though it has been five years since we lived there. I have pastoral friends who complain about meeting me for coffee in that neighborhood because it takes us so long to walk back to our cars for all the people who stop and want to talk to their pastor. The incarnational result is the greatest reason for bi-vocational thinking, and it reveals the divine genius of the bi-vocational church-funding model seen in Scripture.

Friends and Family

Another funding model for church planting that is seen in the New Testament is collecting support from a small circle of friends and family. Jesus had the support of Mary, Martha, and Lazarus, and Paul had Aquila and Priscilla. In alignment with this funding form, all of our Seattle pastors have reached out to their friends and family to help them pay for the food and site rental. Between the offering bucket that is in the room, the pastor's and lead team's tithe into poverty, and the monthly support from friends and family, the monthly budget is met. Sometimes things get tight, but the New Testament patterns of funding for church planting still work.

Financial Deserts

However, all of the talk about New Testament funding approaches does not cancel another important scriptural truth: there will be financial deserts. I would love to say I have the full mind of Christ on this topic, but I don't. However, I have observed several things about deserts because we have been in so many of them. First, everyone went through deserts, and it did not mean we were doing something wrong or were on the wrong path. Second, the greater the promised land we pursued, the longer the desert that led to it. Third, deserts helped us become fully convinced of the Lord's desire and ability to care for us. Fourth, that dependency on him was not irresponsible, but rather, intelligent. Fifth, deserts taught us not to fear bad financial news. Sixth, deserts showed us how to travel light. Seventh, deserts proved to us that the human calculator and the God calculator do not work the same way, but they both work. Eighth, deserts taught us to expect the unexpected, and that God was brilliant at making a way where there was no way.

Never discount what God wants to teach you in the desert. It was in the desert that God showed Moses the map of Israel's escape route from slavery; it was in the desert that God showed Moses the principle of divine provision; and it was in the desert that God showed Moses that he would stop at nothing to make a way where there was no way for his people. These are all lessons that every pioneer church leader needs to know in heart. Our minds know the stories, but we need deserts to implant the truth of them in our hearts so as to reshape our emotions. Only deserts can do that.

Last month we were in a serious financial desert; this month, not so much. If six months from now another one shows up, we won't be surprised or dismayed. We won't be surprised because deserts happen to everyone from time to time, and we won't be dismayed because none of us, or our dinner communities, has missed a meal in any of the previous deserts. So why would God

forget to send us the daily bread now? Such is the attitude of desert-ready leaders.

The Provider

While we cannot control deserts, we have been given
some authority to affect how resources flow. There is an
interesting Old Testament account about the children
of Israel being attacked in the desert (Exodus 17:8–13).
While the attack was understandable because of the
large Israeli population moving through an inhabited
area, it was Moses' response to it that is mysterious. He
went up to a hill that overlooked the battle, took his
staff, and held it over his head. When he did that, Israel
began to prevail, but when he got tired and put his arms
down, Israel started to falter. So obvious was the cause
and effect of Moses' action that his companions began
holding up his arms so he could maintain that posture
until the battle was won.

What was that posture? His rod represented the
inbreaking power of God, and it was up to him to get God
into the situation by holding up the rod. Touching that
rod to the rock caused water to flow and save the people
from dehydration; raising that rod against the Red Sea
caused it to part and save the people from Egypt's retal-
iatory attack; pointing that rod caused water to turn to
blood and hail to fall from the sky to save the people
from further slavery. That rod was God's way of autho-
rizing Moses to call down divine resources of all kinds
as they made their way out of bondage and through the
greatest desert of their lives. As a leader, do you know
how to invite God's provisions into your deserts?

One particular desert a while back stretched so long that I felt I would be swallowed up by the financial stress and overwhelming fear. As I sat in the darkness of my living room very early one morning (because I couldn't sleep anyway), this scripture of Moses holding up the rod came to my mind. I meditated on it for a while, and acknowledged that I had not been holding up the rod that called for the inbreaking power of the Provider over our situation.

I then sensed the Lord tell me something that made me laugh out loud: "Put me in, coach." That was something I used to say to my basketball coach in college after I had gotten a rest on the bench. And now God was asking me to put him in! I wondered what I had ever done to take him out of the game. Yet, the point is very clear in the Moses-holding-the-rod story: the authority to get God into the situation rested in Moses' hands. Most leaders have not stopped to consider the fact that God awaits their word to get into the game. Also in this divine download moment, my heart understood that the reason I was being eaten up by financial stress and fear was because I was not ushering God back into the situation by holding up my arms and proclaiming him the Provider over the lack that was presenting itself in our desert. I had stewed and worried and crunched the budget with the human calculator until I was exhausted, but I hadn't walked through our dinner churches and put the Provider into the game. I had prayed for his help, but that wasn't the same as doing the Moses thing and proclaiming the Provider was Lord over our desert. I started doing it that day, and predictably, the fear and financial stress dissipated. And, of course, financial provision started to flow into our desert.

I don't claim to understand the interplay in the heavenlies between the invited authority of God and the prince of the power of the air. But I do know that when I stopped praying, begging, and budgeting, and started proclaiming the Provider all over our desert, something unexplainable happened in our desert. I now acknowledge that, for some reason, I have been given the authority to invite God and his resources into our situation, and I now insist he get into the game as if it's one of my daily pastoral duties. After that experience, deserts have never looked the same again.

The Harvest Prayer

Jesus' harvest prayer also changed and matured our team's view of money and supply. The text in Matthew 9 reveals that Jesus had been healing long lines of people for quite some time. As he looked at the crowds of the poor before him, milling about like lost sheep, he told his disciples to "pray to the Lord who is in charge of the harvest; ask him to send more workers into his fields" (v. 38).

What is interesting about this prayer is the compassion it reveals. People who knew they needed a Physician were the very people Jesus looked for, and the harvest on that day was full of people who knew they needed help. He was moved by the mixture of mission and compassion. What a great combination!

But what is even more interesting is that he didn't ask for money. In fact, Jesus never seemed to ask for money from God. The closest he came to teaching people to ask for money was when he taught them to pray, "Give us this day our daily bread" (Matt. 6:11 KJV).

But he then made it clear that, though money issues dominate the minds of unbelievers, the Father already knows about our needs and has designed the earth to supply its inhabitants—be they birds, flowers, or people (Matthew 6:25–33). Many people do not see that God is providing for them every day, but believers should see the blessings that are new every morning. So, the daily bread prayer surely wasn't a longing prayer for money, coming from a languishing soul.

A harvest prayer that does not include requesting money would sure be surprising to church planters and leaders across our land. Money is always the biggest concern. What are we missing when we think money is the big hurdle? And what did Jesus and his young leaders know about supply and resources that caused them to completely overlook the need to pray for money?

The elephant in the room on this issue is how incredibly expensive the traditional church model is to plant and run. Salaries, buildings, utilities, tech tools, advertising, coaching, volunteer training tools, signage, mailers . . . the list goes on and on. I'm quite sure Jesus did not have such a complex list of expenses in mind when he was overlooking the harvest that day. The early church did not have a very complex list either. They met in houses and ate together in the Judeo context, and met in rented halls and ate potluck dinners together in the Gentile context; neither was an expensive ordeal. It was 150 years after Christ before the church owned its first building,[2] and not until the fourth century when expensive budgets for stately buildings, salaries, and sanctuary icons flourished.

While expensive budgets have been the heritage of the church for seventeen hundred years, new expressions of the church are finding wondrous freedom from the overlord of money. Church planters are coming into a time when they feel free to simply cry over the harvests the Lord is showing them and ask, "Lord, send me workers to help me bring this harvest to heaven." Think of it: church planting without money problems. I welcome the day.

Carve It out of the Rock

Another financial attitude that the Lord forged in our hearts came from the early American church. While not Scripture-based, this history resonated with us in a significant way. The early church planters were rugged people who moved into a town with nothing but a call. They did not have a coach, they did not have a funding partner, and they did not have a supporting church in their back pockets. They had nothing but a desire to take people to heaven. They found jobs, opened up storefront churches, worked by day, visited people by night, prayed hard, preached hard, and literally carved their church out of the rock. Jesus added to their sacrifices with miracle after miracle until a church was born, and soon it was becoming a mature expression of Christ in their city.

I am not proposing we go back to the lone gunslinger version of church leadership, but I am reminding us of the rugged attitude that drove churches into existence. Almost every established church in our country began by someone who started with nothing but an indomitable confidence that he was sent, and God was going to help him.

It was from this era of pastors that we drew the courage to leave our comfortable building and walk into secular places with significant social needs to carve a new work from scratch. It was also from this era that the following poem was written, and it became our anthem. May it alter your views about supply, and breathe the same strength into you as it did into us.

> *We the willing,*
>   *led by the unknowing,*
> *are doing the impossible*
>   *for the incapable.*
> *We have done so much*
>   *with so little*
>   *for so long*
> *that we are now qualified*
>   *to do anything*
>   *with nothing.*

CALLING ALL CHURCH PLANTERS

Paul had a vision: A man from Macedonia in northern Greece was standing there, pleading with him, "Come over to Macedonia and help us!"
—Acts 16:9

Most traditional churches in America are waning. The bulk of church researchers now reveal that 85 percent of churches are stalled or declining.[1] Some studies suggest that a full 95 percent are stalled and in decline.[2] This is creating no small frustration among many of our leaders, especially our church planters. After all, if the traditional model is not working any better than this, then what kind of church does a planter plant? Beneath that question is another one: What kind of planter would be capable of church planting among the seculars?

Poison in the Pot

I have been working with church planters a great deal over the past ten years. Accordingly, I have observed some popular leadership ideas that may play well with

traditional approaches, but are actually poisonous to
the fresh expressions of the church that the Spirit is
bringing to the church. If that poison is not counter-
acted, it will kill the dream the Lord has for them.

The first poisonous strain for church planters is
ever-talk and never-plant. There are thousands of
church planters in the batter's circle of Christianity.
The frustrating part is that these potential big hitters
were in the same batter's circle this time last year,
and the year before, and the year before that. They are
stuck in an endless loop of training, preparation, and
waiting. While I am sure that fear is the primary culprit
for this poisoning, it is killing many of the Lord's
dreams for expansion. There is a growing conversation
about decision-making that I find very intriguing for
young leaders. The science of decision-making is now
proposing that any decision that is 80 percent positive
is a fully mature decision and needs to be acted on.[3]
What a benefit would be served to the kingdom of Christ
if our on-deck leaders acknowledged that 80 percent of
their church-plant plans were already made, and moved
directly toward launch. I know that sounds scary, but
it is closer to reality than the 100 percent preplanning
ideal.

While there will always be voices from the established church that would say such an approach is
premature and ill-advised, please remember they have
spent their time in the settled church world. But you
are a pioneer! Frontier leaders must move out with
undersupplied resources and under-answered questions, or they will never conquer new territory. Failing
forward is another interesting factor that is entering the
science of decision-making. This leadership discipline

embraces the idea that many of the hurdles on the innovation path cannot be seen until you jump the previous ones. Thus, it is a waste of time to try to pre-guess what hurdles will present themselves. The science of failing forward teaches that you just have to start and jump whatever hurdles show up. For these reasons and more, church planters by the droves remain on the sidelines. Stop polishing your plans and start something! While this is contrary to the counsel of many church-planting coaches, it would sure be a surprise to the apostle Paul to be handed the timetables and checklists that are commonplace in most church-planting training sessions. After all, it only took him three months to plant a dinner church, train a pastor, and commission elders when he went to Thessalonica.[4]

Another poisonous root in church-plant thinking is the desire to plant a church where the leader wants to raise his or her family. That is not missiological thinking. When looking at the US planting map, we seem to be following a missiology of establishing new works in the places where we already have significant presence.[5] I propose that the Lord's dream for your church plant is probably not in the place where you want to live.

One more thought that is poisoning many leaders is that they are in reaction mode against the waning proclamation version of church. It is one thing to feel a call to a different vision; it is another thing to go "scorched earth" and burn down the relationships and the bridges. Many young church planters are burning up their inheritance that will be needed to invest in their frontline vision. Yes, there will be those who try to devalue the fresh expressions of the church, but don't react by flushing them. Their warnings are merely the old wineskins cracking and squeezing. That is something our Master said would happen. This is a time for patience, patience, and more patience. You are going to need your inheritance one day to resource your calling, and probably before you hit mile marker two.

Yet another poison that is affecting large volumes of church planters is the idea of planting the church of your dreams. We have all attended many churches and intentionally or unwittingly made a list of things that would define our perfect church. This perfect-church list has caused church planters by the droves to go into new areas to plant their version of perfect church. They expect that because it is so cool, people will flock to it like crazy on the merits of its innovation and pure awesomeness. The only problem with perfect-church approaches is we are called to do church for the social circle we are called to, not do church for what we want.

Our Seattle leaders had to learn this in a big way. We had been doing church the way we found meaningful for many years; our kind of worship, our kind of décor, our kind of preaching, and our kind of everything else. Our church was a collection of all the elements that we wanted. The fiery truth is that while we were doing exactly what we wanted, we were shrinking. Our community could not make it any clearer that our version of church did not resonate with them. We finally stumbled our way into doing church in a manner that made sense to our Seattle neighbors. It was really different; if that is what resonated with them, no wonder they didn't want to join us.

Of this I am very sure: your version of church will only make sense for churchgoers who are exactly like you. And it is poison to the Lord's dream for you to insist on doing that version of church.

There is an annual event in Seattle called the Lard Butt 1K. It is a one-kilometer run that serves donuts and beer and sets up concert stages every few hundred yards along the way. Obviously, this is not for the serious marathoner, but for a different kind of runner. What an example to us. Our approaches to church will always be for the marathoners who are invested in the gospel. But as planters, we are called to reach the seculars, who are not invested in the gospel; they are only interested in talking about it. Our favorite ways of doing church assume investment; their way of doing church assumes interest. Their way of doing church will look as sacrilegious as the Lard Butt event looks to a serious marathoner, but if that is where they need to start, so be it. We church planters are there to do church for them, not us. Anything else is poisonous to the Lord's dream.

There is another assumption in the church-planting world that a charismatic persona holding a microphone, standing in a spotlight on a polished stage, and emanating from multiple big screens is needed for churches to thrive. I tread lightly here, because there are some with charismatic gifts whom the Lord elevates to such a platform. However, it is the exception, not the rule. I applaud the leaders who find themselves on a big stage reluctantly but do so anyway out of obedience. I applaud their honesty when they admit that their ministry will have very little effect on the lost because they are leading from a template that can't rescue sinners well. I applaud them when they consider it a sacrifice to teach large rooms full of the already-saved. And I really applaud them when they assume a position of being a supply line for those planters who actually get to go to the front lines, where Christ is enveloping seculars into his family. But for any leader to long for the big stage—that is poisonous to the Lord's favorite dream for them.

Twenty-some years ago, I went through a clinical burnout in my ministry. Through counseling, a sabbatical, and prayer, I got down to the reason for my burnout: I was secretly longing to be a large-church pastor with large-church influence. Once I saw that longing for what it was—a cruel taskmaster—I started confessing that desire and making room for the Lord's dream, and the burnout depression dispersed. I was being poisoned by a big-church longing, and was left too unhealthy in my soul to embrace the Lord's dream—which actually turned out to be a pretty cool one.

Still another poison that flows through the veins of planters is an attitude of "show me the money." Sometimes this attitude manifests in an insistence on a good salary; other times it shows up as a lust for big-pocketed financial partners to pony up the cash for one's plant ideas. Some planters even court a version of martyrdom by saying, "If my family and I are willing to sacrifice by doing a new church, then others better step up so I don't have to face financial challenges!" But what if Jesus wants you to be bi-vocational and earn the majority of your living from a neighborhood job? Or what if he wants you to go into a secular desert, where supplies are limited, to retrieve lost people? I am disturbed by the number of church planters who simply will not advance toward their calling until the money is paid up front. I am sure glad the early leaders did not think that way, or we'd have to reduce the four Gospels and the book of Acts down to about a paragraph.

Earl Book, a great leader from our past, used to ask church planters, "What would you do for the Lord with your last five dollars?" What an interesting question. It suggests that if you are a church planter, you may be deciding how your last five dollars best serves the mission a lot. Is being on your last five dollars okay with you? Any version of "show me the money" is different from the mind-set of Christianity's first church planters, and it is pure poison.

The Stalwart Breed of Planter

A final form of poison that is particularly deadly to church planting has to do with soft hands, and by that I mean uncalloused work ethics. Church planting is rugged work; if it is not infused with a never-say-die attitude, it will be a failed venture. Let me be quick to say, you can't judge a book by its cover on this topic of soft hands. I know of big, bold, and boisterous personalities that wilted under the pressure of wrestling lost people away from wolves. And I know of soft-spoken and mild-mannered leaders who can arise with a lion-like roar when Jesus sends them into harm's way on a rescue mission.

One of our pastors, named Luke, a man with as mild a personality as you can imagine, was walking down the sidewalk of his neighborhood one afternoon when two guys got into a fist fight. The bystanders cleared away from the flailing and started recording the event

on their phones. When Luke realized that both of the
fighters attended his dinner church on Wednesday
nights, he marched right into the middle of them, pushed
them apart, stared into their eyes until they stopped
swinging, and then said, "This is not who we are!"
Both fighters took a step back, nodded in agreement,
then turned and walked away in opposite directions.
The onlookers were stunned at Luke's mastery of the
moment, but then again, they didn't know who he was
in that neighborhood.

Luke then turned his eyes on the crowd and said,
"Put your stupid iPhones away. Would you want
someone videoing your worst moments?" And with
that, the amateur videographers put their phones in
their pockets and slunk away. It was a God moment for
sure, similar to when Jesus faced down the crowd who
wanted to stone the lady caught in adultery (John 8:1–11).
That was stalwart.

The scariest thing in the wilderness is not the wolf,
but rather, the protective shepherd with a stick in his
hand and the rescue of sheep on his mind. Pastors are
called shepherds for many reasons, but perhaps the
most dramatic is their willingness to square off with
the wolves that would destroy the work of the gospel in
the sheep they are sent to rescue.

With fresh expressions of church planting
developing, many of our pastors will be entering environments that are not as safe and sane as our sanitized
Sunday-morning churches. Our leaders would do
well to embrace the shepherd's role, which includes
defending their sheep against wolves. Not all people are
sheeplike; some are goatlike, and others are wolflike.
Our pastors have been trained to embrace the sheep

who are reaching for help, tolerate the goats who are just there eating food, and square off with the wolves, because that is their job. And because Jesus, the Great Lion, lives within you, you are the scariest one in the neighborhood. That is stalwart church planting.

Church planters are sent into deserts to change them. According to Psalm 84, it is the heritage of God's family to turn deserts into oases with pools, green grass, and trees. But for this to happen, someone has to go when it is just an undersupplied desert and call down the kingdom of God to break into that place. Jesus will authorize the kingdom download if we will walk in and go to work as if we actually believe we will change that place. There are church planters who offer soft hands to the Lord; they can only serve the Judeos, who already grasp much of the gospel and church world. Then there are church planters who are a stalwart breed that offer calloused hands; they can be sent into the secular deserts and do church for people with no church understanding at all. America doesn't need more of the soft-hand leaders, but it sure needs hoards of the stalwart breed. And I believe Jesus can breathe a stalwart spirit into anyone.

Something beyond Proclamation

Church planters have assumed the Sunday-morning proclamation template for the past five centuries, but that form of church is waning. This is the time in human history when innovators arise and find new ways to thrive. This is the time when church planters are needed more than ever, but not to do more of the same. They are now needed to invent the future.

We have obsessed over Sunday-morning proclamation gatherings and organizational systems for so
long, we have forgotten how to do honest missiological
work in our own neighborhoods. Leaders would be well
served by digging beneath the discussions of relevance
based on speaking content, worship styles, sanctuary
décor, branding, and prayer stations. These things all
function on the proclamation template, which was
designed during the Reformation; it is a teaching-based
structure that assumes everyone has a churched understanding and is present for a greater understanding
of Scripture. While that template is very meaningful
for countless Christians, it was not designed to move
people who hold a secular worldview toward faith.
Seculars are now the dominant portion of the population in almost every zip code in America, which is why
the proclamation church is statistically ineffective and
in decline. We need to dig beneath the foundations of
the proclamation church and find new ways of doing
church in which the path to salvation actually starts
where the seculars live. Church planters, lay down your
preconceived notions, get to a quiet place, and let Jesus
dream with you.

Templates and Models

There is a difference between a template of church
and a model of church. Templates are foundational
constructs on which Christian spiritual development
can occur on a wide scale, and the scriptural purposes
of the church can be employed. Models, on the other
hand, are particular variations of church that function
on the foundational template.

During the apostolic era the template was the Jesus dinner table, while the models were the house churches for the Jews and agape churches for the Gentiles. During the Christendom era the template was sacred-space liturgy, while the models were created by each denomination according to its traditions. During the Reformation era, the template has been the proclamation event, while the models that have functioned on the proclamation assumption are numerous—too numerous to list. Templates have a metanarrative nature to them; models are particular and situational.

Today, there are many fresh expressions rising that will become the new models of the church. And because these new expressions are incarnational, there could be as many variations as there are under-gospeled social circles in our land. There is a new template rising too. With the Reformation template clearly waning, another foundation for the church is needed to step into the gap. The rising template is actually a resurgence of the first template: the Jesus dinner table. The reason this template is so needed and timely is its great abilities in evangelism. Different templates through history have revealed different strengths. The use of the dinner table template by the first apostles propelled Christianity from a movement of thousands to a movement of millions in a very short period of time.[6] The table's ability to gather saints and sinners to sit together and talk about Jesus is unparalleled. With Western civilization walking away from the Judeo worldview in favor of secular worldviews, the church desperately needs a template that can embrace the seculars.

I am deeply moved by all of the fresh expressions that are rising and entering new social circles of

America. Bold planters are doing bold reaches, yet how will these new expressions create environments for the divine invitation to occur? Once planters engage their social circles, many are eliminating the proclamation event as a potential way of piloting their newfound friends toward Christ. And yet, even in this postmodern day that is throwing off all metanarratives, an effective template is still needed.

For each leader of these new expressions of the church, I have one question: Where are you placing your Jesus dinner table? There are few places in society where heaven can meet earth in a natural way, and where saints and sinners can sit and hear Jesus' divine invitation together. I know of no other template that has the ability to fuse with the growing number of incarnational models as well as the template the apostles used: the Jesus dinner table. So, where is yours?

Sidewalk Missiology

Missiology is the equal blend of theology and sociology and is the first leadership skill needed by anyone looking to extend the kingdom of God to a new place. But herein lies the problem: most pastors have been trained in theology but not so thoroughly in sociology. We understand the movements of God far better than we understand the movements of people. And yet we are called to "go" to people and draw them to Christ (Matt. 28:19). Thus, missiology is an indispensable discipline in a church leader's tool kit.

Paul and the apostles engaged in serious sociological evaluation in their day, and purposefully stepped into opportunities for the gospel. Evidence of such work peppers the pages of Acts and the Epistles. I particularly like how Paul told Timothy to do the work of an evangelist (2 Timothy 4:5). That was arguably his way of directing Timothy toward missiological insight. Evangelists are those in the five-fold ministry who are called to be among the sinners, observing the ways of the sinners. That is the heartbeat of missiology.

Once we felt compelled into the urban neighborhoods of Seattle, we admitted that we did not understand the people who lived there. I remembered hearing about a missiologist who used to observe the movements of people through their day and ask Jesus to show him where the opportunities were for the gospel within those movements. So, I started taking a lawn chair down to urban neighborhoods, and Jesus and I just watched people come and go. By that simple exercise, I crafted some conclusions for our church plants.

A first realization was what a dumb idea Sunday mornings were; nobody was out and about on Sunday mornings. You could broad slide a truck across any sidewalk in the city at 10:30 a.m., and you wouldn't hit a soul. On the flip side, I observed that at 5:00 on any weeknight, there was a flood of people thronging the sidewalks. Another observation I made was that the sidewalks were full of people for about six blocks, and then the sidewalks went quiet. People were entering these sidewalks from city buses and from their apartments in the stories above to go to the shops and eateries within those six blocks, but not beyond. Thus, I began to understand that cities are primarily filled with walkers and bus riders. For suburbanites who are accustomed to the driver's identity, that is an important distinction to consider. Finally, I began to see how many people in these walking villages were poor and lonely. The homeless were obvious because they were asking for donations from every corner, but the working poor was a far larger group, and the older, single people were a surprisingly large group too.

All of these observations culminated and created an understanding that the front doors of our cities are located in its walking villages at dinnertime. And if we were doing church in a community space that's in the middle of a walking circle, we would have the attention of thousands of people, and the poor and the lonely would be present. These lawn chair observations became the stuff that the Lord used to compel us toward rebirthing the ancient dinner church; we were doing the work of a missiologist.

It would do the American church well to engage in some good old-fashioned sociological work on the way we do church, when we do church, and where the opportunities for the gospel exist in the social circles that inhabit our neighborhoods. A serious missiological reflection would change almost every church in some dramatic ways. Our challenge is not a theological one nearly as much as it is a sociological one. Some are throwing their hands up in despair as though America is just not interested in the gospel, but that is not the issue. If the dinner churches in Seattle and across the country prove anything, they reveal that secular Americans are not done with Christianity, but they are done with "churchianity."

Urban Cities—Endless Opportunities

The church-to-population ratio in large cities is disturbing. Most urban cities in the United States have four times fewer churches than any other location in the country.[7] While that might sound unimpressive at first glance, it actually reveals a steep abandonment of the exact places where the largest number of Americans live. What this means for my home city of Seattle is that my denominational tribe would need to immediately plant twenty-five of our churches to equal the ratios in all the rest of the state. We could not abandon our largest population centers more directly than if we had set an intentional goal to do so.

The greatest reason our churches are waning in large cities is due to urbanization. When apartment buildings replace single-family houses, a population shift occurs and single people replace families. This explains the decline in our urban churches; our family-based congregations, with family-based assumptions and programs, do not draw the second-life single people who flood into American cities. Once an urban church starts to decline, many move to the suburbs to be with people groups (families) with whom they can identify. The groups that stay experience ongoing declines because they remain family-based churches in an ever-increasing nonfamily location. Year after year of this pressure prompts one church move after another, until only a small church presence remains in the population centers.

Church planters overlook our cities with surprising regularity. Missiologist and researcher Ed Stetzer has noted how it appears to many that God has a special burden for places with hundreds of new homes compared to the inner city with thousands of apartments.[8] This mind-set must change. Urban cities stand in need of the greatest full-court press our church planters can muster. While these leaders will need to adapt to the nonfamily ethos of cities and function in less systematic ways, the fifty urban cities of the United States serve as the greatest mission field in the country, demanding the greatest response possible. Such a response could be initiated by denominational leaders who (1) map citywide church-plant strategies, (2) call forth planters into urban locations, and (3) develop funding partners with nonurban churches by confronting decades of "sovereign church" thinking. While such an initiative would be bold, it would be missiologically appropriate. America's great population centers deserve a significant gospel presence in their neighborhoods.

Dinner Churches in Sore Neighborhoods

The age-old manner of church that filled the pages of the New Testament and marked the first three hundred years of church history still draws the kinds of people it did in those first centuries—the widows, the orphans, the sick, and the strangers. During the apostolic era, Christianity exploded from twenty-five thousand to more than twenty million, and the majority of that growth occurred among those living at the bottom of the economic ladder.[9] The lesson from early church history is that whenever the church thrived with "the least of these," it functioned as a dinner church. For church planters to consider doing church in a way that understands the sociological realities of the poor is an important meditation. To plant a socially engaged model like a dinner church in the middle of the sorest neighborhood in their town will likely produce some very fast and surprising results.

As noted before, dinner churches not only gather the poor and the isolated populations; they also draw the Samaritans and the humanitarians who live near their locations. In one of his famous parables, Jesus highlighted the Samaritan who was willing to help the fallen man, while the religious types were too busy rushing to church (Luke 10:30–37). Many Samaritans exist in every neighborhood, and when they see how a dinner church is lifting broken people, they become intrigued and long to be involved. These Samaritans become another sociogroup that predictably joins the dinner church gatherings.

Steve Sjogren, founding pastor of Vineyard Community Church in Cincinnati, observed that throughout history, whenever the church has reached for the people nobody wants, they end up with the people that everybody wants.[10] Dinner churches find that this phenomenon repeats itself in their stories with enough regularity that the Samaritans soon become a third of their weekly attenders, and we end up taking as many people to heaven who showed up to serve as be served. Dinner church leaders would do well to anticipate the help of the humanitarians in the form of millennials in their church plants. The Samaritans, the humanitarians, and the millennials are coming, and they will be more intrigued with the person of Jesus and his dinner churches than most leaders can imagine.

Macedonian Calls

Scripture reveals a chapter in the life of the apostle Paul when he tried to extend the gospel into Asia, but the Spirit blocked him. Soon after, he had a vision of a Macedonian man waving him to come there, and Paul made haste to respond (Acts 16:6–10). The church-growth movement of the late twentieth century moved leaders to think in terms of regional approaches, automobile-accessible locations, demographics, branding, and strategies. It is not surprising that the idea of the Macedonian call became viewed as "primitive." Interestingly, however, I increasingly hear of church planters receiving Macedonian visions in the night that call and draw them into neighborhoods they would never otherwise choose. For a church planter to be waved into a specific neighborhood by the Spirit himself is a wonderful leadership experience. Certainly, there is nothing wrong with doing church for drivers in suburban locations; that is, unless the Spirit is trying to call you to do church for the walkers and bus riders in a challenged neighborhood.

I am saddened by the years our Seattle pastoral team wasted in strategy sessions and brand building, which made us unable to see the Spirit's hand waving us into nearby neighborhoods. We were as well trained in strategic thinking and marketing as any of our ministerial contemporaries, but somehow the Spirit longed to wrestle our attention away from regional visions to see the sore neighborhoods in our city that beckoned us to come to them.

The first breakthrough occurred in a neighborhood located sixty blocks south of our church campus. I felt such a strange presence every time I drove through that neighborhood that I finally pulled over to the curb and asked the Lord what was going on. While I did not realize at first it was a Macedonian call, I soon figured it out. Over the next few months, the Spirit put us together with Christian businesspeople from that neighborhood who had been praying for decades that Jesus would send a church to them. Conversations with these people made our Macedonian call throb even louder. It was there, within a block of where I pulled over my car, that we planted our first dinner church. Since then we have planted seven more, all of which were preceded by a similar Macedonian-like experience. Not one of them began as a result of strategic thinking.

The Spirit is still beckoning church planters into neighborhoods of Christ's choosing. There exists no greater guarantee of success than to know we are going where he wants rather than where we want to raise our kids. Recovering the expectation of a Macedonian call is a critical missiological first step for our desert-ready church planters. Some great open doors exist for church planting in America, but most of them are not where the majority of planters are looking. In fact, the best opportunities are probably in the exact opposite direction from where most church plants are being planned. I predict that sore neighborhoods, urban cities, Macedonian calls, and socially engaged models such as dinner churches will be the places and approaches that our stalwart planters will use to forge the future of the church in upcoming decades.

THE FAMILY RESCUE BUSINESS

"If a man has a hundred sheep and one of them
gets lost, . . . Won't he leave the ninety-nine others
in the wilderness and go to search for the one that
is lost until he finds it? . . . Or suppose a woman
has ten silver coins and loses one. Won't she . . .
sweep the entire house and search carefully until
she finds it? . . . A man had two sons. . . .
[The] younger son packed . . . and moved to
a distant land, and there he wasted all his
money in wild living. . . . When he finally
came to his senses, . . . he returned home
. . . And while he was still a long way off, his
father saw him coming . . . he ran to his son,
embraced him, and kissed him. . . . His father
said . . . 'He was lost, but now he is found!'"
—Luke 15:4, 8, 11, 13, 17, 20, 31–32

There are many theologies related to the kingdom of
God, but not all of them hold the same level of importance. Jesus told numerous parables, but only once did
he tell three stories back to back to emphasize the same

point. I believe he reserved these compounding parables to emphasize one kingdom theme that was more important than the rest: rescue! The lost sheep, the lost coin, and the lost son all share one word: *lost* (Luke 15). The rescue of the lost is the preeminent theology of all Scripture. In fact, the theme of rescue is the most repeated idea throughout both Old Testament and New Testament verses.[1] That God's family is in the rescue business is the easiest theological position to argue.

However, much of the American church has forgotten the primacy of the rescue mission. Researching church websites, it appears that many are in the teaching business, or the Bible business, or the family-building business, or the growth business, or the discipleship business, or big business—and some are even in the "we-don't-know-what-we-are" business. Over the years, the churches I have led have been in several of these businesses too. Ouch. All of this aside, the volume of Scripture makes it clear that God's family only owns one business: the rescue business.

Gospel Explained as Rescue

The life of Christ revealed what was on his mind the most, and it was the salvation of the world. From his repeated stories, to his repeated salvific works, to his death on the cross, Jesus was clearly focused on the rescue business. I love the story in Luke 2 where Joseph and Mary had to double back to find young Jesus after leaving him in Jerusalem by mistake. When they located him in the temple, talking theology with the leaders, Jesus' defense was, "Didn't you know that I would need to be about my Father's business?" (v. 49, paraphrased).

This story begs the question: And what business was that? Jesus answered that question with the way he spent his life.

John the Baptist first identified Jesus as the Savior of the world. The first apostles referred to him in the same way as they established the first church. Many people hear the title "Savior," and think it refers primarily to his work on the cross. But *Savior* speaks to more than his signing the new covenant with his blood; it also speaks to the God-family calling, and it speaks to the church's calling, and it speaks to each Christian's calling. Let's pause to hear that title again in its fullness: "the Savior of the world." The term *Savior* created an earthly rescue image for the first-century Jew, while for the Western Christian in the twenty-first century, it has a heavenly placement image. If we wanted to feel Jesus' title the way the first church did, we would do well to use "the Rescuer of the world."

The gospel was explained in rescue terms through the first centuries of Christian history as well. In AD 140, Irenaeus penned the ransom explanation of atonement, which created an imagery of a generous Savior who is willing to pay a large sum to free a person from oppression.[2] This metaphor of the gospel was the dominant explanation until the eleventh century, when Anselm proposed the satisfaction explanation, which was an egregious departure from the ransom metaphor. It portrayed God as so offended by sin that he demanded satisfaction from sinners in the form of penance. Then, and *only* then, would he grant them salvation. Fast-forward to the 1500s and Calvin's penal substitution explanation of the gospel started replacing Anselm's imagery, casting the drama of redemption as a court scene. Calvin's narrative of salvation went something like this: mankind is brought into the courtroom charged with sin; mankind then has the opportunity to confess their sin; then the divine gavel falls, declaring them guilty—but just then, Jesus walks into the courtroom and takes mankind's place, and is led out of the courtroom by the bailiff to serve mankind's sentence. Now, don't get me wrong, I hold great reverence for substitutionary atonement as first modeled by the sheep taking Isaac's place on Abraham's altar. But penal substitution has welded punishment ("penal") together with substitution and created a different sound. In fact, both of the recent explanations of the gospel set a very different tone from the one that guided the church for the first one thousand years; the gospel tones of an angry God and a guilty sinner have eclipsed the original tone of a rescuing Savior. It is little wonder why the present-day church has forgotten about the God-family rescue business.

Not All People Are Equal

If Jesus' story about the lost sheep, the lost coin, and the lost son say anything to us, it is that not all people demand an equal response from the Rescuer. Lost people are in the greatest danger, and are simply in greater need of rescue. Jesus never apologized for spending large portions of his time with the sick, the poor, and the broken. In fact, as noted earlier, he specifically looked for those who already knew they needed a physician (Mark 2:17). This is something church planters need to consider when developing their people targets for their new plants.

Some church leaders try to imagine a kingdom where everything is fair, including the Lord's attention. But Jesus just did not look at it that way. He made it clear that his first attention would be with the lost, the broken, and the estranged. Jesus' presence will pour into the circles of humanity that need him most. This gives rise to the increased presence of Christ in our dinner church rooms. He is there in great volume because the broken are there in great numbers.

When Rescuers Don't Rescue

In the first few months of opening our first dinner church, we began to feel a frustration within our souls. We were doing the right thing, but there was a growing conflict in us. In our efforts to be sensitive to our friends, we were toning down the worship and the preaching to easy themes and approaches. But what we were actually doing was frustrating the Rescuer that lived within us. Our theology of rescue hadn't been fully captured yet, so we were under-practiced at working in rhythm with the Rescuer of the world. We had invited the Rescuer to live within us, but we were not letting that same Rescuer out to do his thing—rescue the perishing. In time, we began to understand how to flow with Jesus, how to observe prevenient grace at work in a sinner's life, and how to point out that prevenient grace which Jesus is already pouring into their lives. All to say, we figured out how to stop frustrating him as we sit with the unsaved night after night.

There are Christian leaders across the land who are frustrating the Rescuer that lives in them. The Lord is in the rescue business, but many of our churches are pursuing other forms of spiritual-sounding businesses. When this happens, the Rescuer of the world is grieved, his rescue plans are frustrated, and Christian leaders feel stressed in their ministries. When rescuers don't rescue, the Rescuer is displaced. This is worth some serious meditation for the American church.

Churches Structured for Training

Organizational systems frustrate the Rescuer as much under-practiced leaders and Christians do. It appears that most of our churches are engineered to download scriptural information while keeping our Christians hanging out with each other. Proclamation churches are structured for training, not rescue. In most traditional churches there is neither time nor place for the activity of rescue to be practiced by the average church family.

We diagnosed this problem in our church long before we received the dinner table vision. Under my fine pastoral leadership, our people were kept so busy coming back and forth to hear me teach that they had no time to develop any non-Christian friendships, much less have any confidence to share the gospel with anyone if they did. They were under-practiced in the divine calling of rescue. When we came to terms with that, I started praying for the Lord to help us create a Great Commission environment that would be a regular part of our weekly calendar so my people could practice rescuing the lost alongside Christ. How exciting it was when we opened our first dinner church and realized that our people now had a place to practice rescue and actually engage in rescue—and it was baked right into the weekly calendar! It did not take long for that Great

Commission environment to change us. We went from merely having a weekly Great Commission gathering to *existing* for our Great Commission gatherings. Jesus reframed our entire church organization around his rescue mission.

Called to Risk, but Accustomed to Comfort

Rescue is risk. Consider the fireman who runs into a burning building to collect an infant from the top floor, or a coast guard swimmer who jumps into the pounding surf to save a drowning person. These rescuers are throwing themselves into harm's way for the sake of preserving life. While the idea of working beside the Rescuer might sound like an adventurous form of Christianity, it also suggests a degree of risk.

The problem is that most churches have built their crowds on the promise of comfort. Our nice buildings, our plush pews, our colorful children's bounce houses, and the climbing wall in the youth chapel all paint a picture of a comfortable learning environment for the whole family. The only risk in attending most churches is that a wide-flinging door might dent our car in the parking lot. Other than that, things are quite comfortable.

Our theological brothers from other countries are seriously worried about the American church, and our inability to grasp the sacrificial faith. I heard a United Kingdom seminary leader say he was really glad that his daughter, who lived in Los Angeles, did not have any children. He questioned, "Who would train my grandchild in the sacrificial faith? Your churches? With your ball pits, bounce houses, and climbing walls?"[3] It was an interesting reality check for the eight of us American pastors in attendance. I am very sure that people who have been discipled in the sacrificial faith are likelier to follow Jesus into risk environments than are people who have been discipled in the comfort faith. Perhaps this is the reason our church planters are quick to overlook the urban settings and the sore neighborhoods and, instead, target the sanitized suburban locations over and over again. If Jesus is in the rescue business, then we are in the rescue business. And if we are called to rescue, we are called to risk.

Christians need to be urged. If the rescue business is going to be human resourced anytime soon, leaders need to call their people forth and commission them to the task of rescue. Bold pastors need to stand in front of their congregations and compel them to leave their "go-to-church" Christianity behind and, instead, enter into their "rescuer Christian" calling. While this will probably take many compelling invitations to offset decades of comfort-based assumptions, it is the path back to the family rescue business, and the people of God need to be called forth to walk it.

The Leadership Challenge

Not only will our Christians need to be called into the rescue business; our churches will have to be rewired to embrace the rescue calling. With 85 percent of America's churches stalled or in decline, getting everyone refocused on rescue is urgent. This is the leadership challenge in our age.

For this kind of rescue formation to occur, the leaders must learn to work beside the Rescuer themselves.

That means that the idea of "fifty hours in the church office" might need to be rethought. One cannot learn to be a rescuer when one's time is spent with the already-rescued.

Once a leader has gotten his or her rescuer mojo back, that leader can then go to work on the rescue-formation of their people. This is more than encouraging them to go evangelize their neighbors; it is actually restoring a viable redemption plan that the congregations can engage in. This is not the same thing as crafting a mission statement; it is crafting an effective strategy of evangelism in which the congregation can cooperate with and know their role within it.

Previous generations had a clearer understanding of the redemption plan of their church. The redemption strategy of the parish church was to engage their people in the social needs of the neighborhood during the week and worship on Sundays. The redemption strategy of the storefront churches before the 1950s was to disciple the saints on Sundays and call evangelists to win the lost. My father served as a pastor during this era, and he would call an evangelist twice a year to hold nightly salvation meetings. It was the church's role to invite their unsaved neighbors to those evening soul-winning meetings. Once there were thirty-five new converts, the evangelist would leave, and then the congregation would be instructed to parent the new ones into the faith. In that way the church worked together to redeem seventy people per year—which was my father's goal. The redemption strategy of the evangelical churches of the 1950s was to have worship on Sunday mornings and have evangelistic services on Sunday evenings. The Christians cooperated with their church's evangelism plans by inviting their unsaved friends on Sunday nights. The redemption strategy of the church-growth movement starting in the 1960s was to hire winsome preachers and excellent musicians to make Sunday-morning gatherings a compelling event for the lost. The Christians' role was to now bring their unsaved friends to that well-rehearsed evangelistic event.

However, in the late 1980s, the church-growth strategy started to become statistically ineffective in evangelism. Though it continued to draw the saved to their ranks, it was pronounced dead as an evangelism strategy. Since then, the onus of redemption has shifted to the individual Christians to evangelize their friends as they work and walk in the world, exercising personal evangelism. While that has had varying levels of success over the years, dependent on the confidence of the individual Christian, the idea of clear redemption strategies has faded from most congregations. In fact, most churches have forgotten that there is supposed to be a viable redemption plan that each member of the church family understands and can cooperate with. The identity of a church that is in the rescue business has become eclipsed by the "going-to-church business," and clarity of mission has become difficult to find for many leaders.

This is now where the leadership challenge lies: (1) to restore the assumption that each church should have a redemption strategy that everyone engages in, (2) to create a redemption plan that fits their people and their neighborhood, (3) to establish a Great Commission environment in the weekly life of the church that is every bit as significant and attended as the weekly worship gathering, and (4) to call their people back into the Christian rescue business and take their place in that church's specific redemption plan. This is a huge leadership task, but such is the way back out of the fog bank that most churches live in.

While some pastors have the skill set to restore a viable redemption plan for their congregation, most will need help from consultants and coaches to accomplish it. Despite the difficulty of the leadership challenge, it must be done. Rescue is the business of the church, so stop at nothing to get your people proficient at it again.

CONCLUSION

Christianity is the greatest rescue project the world has ever seen. The Father, the Son, and the Holy Spirit have committed to keep the rescue mission at the center of their attention, which means that the church is assigned to keep it at the center of our attention as well. Decisions that have been made in the heavenlies directly inform decisions that are to be made here on earth. Should the church become misaligned, and push any initiative ahead of rescue, the family business will start to fail. However, despite the multitudes of declining churches in America, mission failure is not what I see on the horizon.

The ancient dinner church that has been asleep for more than thirteen hundred years is waking up again. The Jesus dinner table is starting to provide a significant template for the church. This is so timely because if the church needs anything, it's to get proficient at evangelism again, and that was the primary strength of the historic Jesus dinner table. The poor, the lost, and the lonely who fill the sore neighborhoods of our nation are in deep need of a resurgence of the dinner table theology, where sinner and saint can sit together and hear the Savior say:

"Look! I stand at the door and knock.
If you hear my voice and open the door, I will come in,
and we will share a meal together as friends."
(Rev. 3:20)

NOTES

Chapter 1: The Day We Realized We Had Cancer

1. Jim Cymbala, "We Got to Change up the Game" (lecture, Orlando Convention Center, Orlando, FL, August 6, 2014).

2. Quoted in Graydon Snyder, Julian Hills, and Richard Gardner, *Common Life in the Early Church* (Harrisburg, PA: Trinity Press International, 1998), 141.

3. Quoted in Ed Stetzer, *Planting New Churches in a Postmodern Age* (Nashville, TN: Broadman & Holman Publishers, 2003), 10.

4. Seattle is known to be the most secular city in the nation. Church pollster David Olson has suggested that doubling the church attenders in any given city would account for the de-churched population, and thus define the Judeos—leaving the remainder with no church background (i.e., seculars). Based on that formula, Seattle consists of 10 percent Judeos (5 percent church attenders, 5 percent de-churched) and 90 percent holding a secular worldview. David Olson, "12 Surprising Facts about the American Church, 2008 Edition," The American Church Research Project, June 1, 2013, http://www.theamericanchurch.org.

Chapter 2: The First Dinner Church

1. Robert Stallman, "Divine Hospitality in the Pentateuch: A Metaphorical Perspective on God as Host" (PhD diss., University of Michigan, 1999), 272, https://eagle.northwestu.edu/faculty/bob-stallman/files/2011/03/7.pdf.
2. John Perry, *Exploring the Evolution of the Lord's Supper in the New Testament*, Exploring Scripture Series (Kansas City, MO: Sheed & Ward, 1994), 4.
3. Ibid.
4. Graydon Snyder, Julian Hills, and Richard Gardner, *Common Life in the Early Church* (Harrisburg, PA: Trinity Press International, 1998), 30, 141.
5. Ibid., 142.
6. Ibid., 141.
7. Perry, *Exploring the Evolution of the Lord's Supper in the New Testament*, 9.
8. Ibid., 12.
9. Kenneth Leech, *Experiencing God: Theology as Spirituality*, 1st US ed. (San Francisco: Harper & Row, 1985), 268.
10. Christine D. Pohl, *Making Room: Recovering Hospitality as a Christian Tradition* (Grand Rapids, MI: W. B. Eerdmans, 1999), 21–22.
11. Ibid., 14.
12. Snyder, Hills, and Gardner, *Common Life in the Early Church,* 60.
13. Ralph P. Martin, *Worship in the Early Church*, rev. ed. (Grand Rapids, MI: Eerdmans, 1974), 122.
14. Perry, *Exploring the Evolution of the Lord's Supper in the New Testament*, v.
15. James F. White, *A Brief History of Christian Worship* (Nashville, TN: Abingdon Press, 1993), 26.
16. Pohl, *Making Room,* 32.
17. Ibid., 31.
18. Snyder, Hills, and Gardner, *Common Life in the Early Church*, 89.
19. Pohl, *Making Room*, 41.

Chapter 3: Rebirth

1. James F. White, *A Brief History of Christian Worship* (Nashville, TN: Abingdon Press, 1993), 28.
2. Michael Green, *Evangelism in the Early Church*, rev. ed. (Grand Rapids, MI: W. B. Eerdmans Pub., 2004), 255.
3. Ibid., 256.
4. Ibid.
5. Graydon Snyder, Julian Hills, and Richard Gardner, *Common Life in the Early Church* (Harrisburg, PA: Trinity Press International, 1998), 105.
6. Christine D. Pohl, *Making Room: Recovering Hospitality as a Christian Tradition* (Grand Rapids, MI: W. B. Eerdmans, 1999), 46.
7. Snyder, Hills, and Gardner, *Common Life in the Early Church,* 107.
8. Ibid., 187.

Chapter 4: Preaching to Sinners

1. Michael Green, *Evangelism in the Early Church*, rev. ed. (Grand Rapids, MI: W. B. Eerdmans Pub., 2004), 98.
2. Jim Heugel, "The Reformation" (lecture, Northwest University, Kirkland, WA, February 15, 2011).
3. Graydon Snyder, Julian Hills, and Richard Gardner, *Common Life in the Early Church* (Harrisburg, PA: Trinity Press International, 1998), 142.
4. Heugel, "The Reformation" (lecture).

Chapter 5: The Healer

1. Graydon Snyder, Julian Hills, and Richard Gardner, *Common Life in the Early Church* (Harrisburg, PA: Trinity Press International, 1998), 141.
2. David Lim, "Holy Spirit in the Church" (lecture, Christian Resource Institute, Kissimmee, FL, July 25, 2010).

Chapter 6: The Message of Food

1. Ben Witherington, *Making a Meal of It: Rethinking the Theology of the Lord's Supper* (Waco, TX: Baylor University Press, 2007), 23.
2. Brennan Manning, *The Ragamuffin Gospel: Good News for the Bedraggled, Beat-Up, and Burnt Out* (Portland, OR: Multnomah, 1990), 59.
3. Christine D. Pohl, *Making Room: Recovering Hospitality as a Christian Tradition* (Grand Rapids, MI: W. B. Eerdmans, 1999), 6.
4. Ben Witherington, *Making a Meal of It: Rethinking the Theology of the Lord's Supper* (Waco, TX: Baylor University Press, 2007), 20.
5. Ibid., 200.
6. John Perry, *Exploring the Evolution of the Lord's Supper in the New Testament*, Exploring Scripture Series (Kansas City, MO: Sheed & Ward, 1994), 97.
7. Ibid., 40.
8. Dick Foth, interview, June 2007.
9. Pohl, *Making Room*, x.

Chapter 7: Table Talk and Natural Evangelism

1. Wonsuk Ma, "An Overview of World Mission" (lecture to a DMin class, OCMS, Oxford, UK, February 21, 2012).
2. Graydon Snyder, Julian Hills, and Richard Gardner, *Common Life in the Early Church* (Harrisburg, PA: Trinity Press International, 1998), 133.

Chapter 8: A Different Path of Salvation

1. Michael Green, *Evangelism in the Early Church*, rev. ed. (Grand Rapids, MI: W. B. Eerdmans Pub., 2004), 167.
2. Acts 19:23 reveals a common use of the phrase "the Way" as a title for the followers of Christ.
3. Thom Rainer and Eric Geiger, *Simple Church* (Nashville, TN: B & H Publishing Group, 2006), 16.

4. *Awan*: iniquity, vanity, sorrow; *asham*: condition
   of guilt, guilt offering, trespass; *amal*: evil, trouble,
   mischief, grievance, wickedness; *awon*: bent, bowed
   down, twisted, perverted; *rasha*: wicked, criminal,
   guilty, hostility to God; *chatta*: punishment for sin; *ra*:
   bad, evil, wicked, sore, unpleasant, wildness; *abar*:
   crossing over from God's covenant, transgression.
5. *Hamartia:* to miss the mark.
6. Daniel Tomberlin, *Encountering God at the Altar:
   The Sacraments in Pentecostal Worship* (Cleveland,
   TN: Pathway Press, 2006), 2; Brian McLaren in
   Leonard Sweet et al., *The Church in Emerging Culture*
   (El Cajon, CA: Zondervan Publishing, 2003), 194.
   McLaren concludes that Luther never invited anyone
   to pray the sinner's prayer, nor did Calvin ever have
   an altar call. Similarly, Augustine never "invited
   anyone to accept Jesus Christ as their personal Lord
   and Savior."
7. Jim Heugel, "Historical Theology" (lecture, Northwest
   University, Kirkland, WA, February 16, 2011).
8. Vinay Samuel, "Mission as Transformation" (DMin
   class lecture, Oxford Center of Mission Studies, Oxford,
   UK, February 23, 2012).
9. Further reflection is needed on getting the church
   ready for the New Gentiles too. While America's
   proclamation-based Sunday gatherings are continuing
   to be effective with the Judeos, they are performing
   poorly with the seculars. Mission-based approaches,
   however, are showing promise at becoming successful
   at taking the New Gentiles to heaven. But this is a
   discussion for another time.
10. Richard Rohr, online Twitter post @RichardRohrOFM.

Chapter 9: Protecting New Vision

1. *Other People's Money*, directed by Norman Jewison,
   Warner Bros., 1991, film.

2. Wonsuk Ma, "The Shelf Life of World Christianity" (lecture, Oxford Center of Mission Studies, Oxford, UK, March 2, 2010).

Chapter 10: Sore Neighborhoods

1. Alan Roxburgh and Scott Boren, *Introducing the Missional Church* (Grand Rapids, MI: Baker Books, 2009), 94.
2. Charles Colson and Harold Fickett, *The Faith: What Christians Believe, Why They Believe It, and Why It Matters* (Grand Rapids, MI: Zondervan Publishers, 2008), 15.
3. David Kinnaman and Gabe Lyons, *Unchristian: What a New Generation Really Thinks about Christianity and Why It Matters* (Grand Rapids, MI: Baker Books, 2007), 87.
4. Christine D. Pohl, *Making Room: Recovering Hospitality as a Christian Tradition* (Grand Rapids, MI: W. B. Eerdmans, 1999), 98.
5. Ibid., 88.
6. Colson and Fickett, *The Faith*, 169.
7. Earl G. Creps, *Off-Road Disciplines: Spiritual Adventures of Missional Leaders*, 1st ed. (San Francisco, CA: Jossey-Bass, 2006), 93.
8. Bill O'Reilly, on *The O'Reilly Show*, aired April 2013.
9. American Factfinder (2006–2008). US Census Bureau. "Seattle, Washington: Selected Economic Characteristics," accessed December 13, 2010, http://factfinder.census.gov/ servlet/ADPTable?_bm=y&-geo_id=16000US5363000&-qr_name=ACS_2009_5YR_G00_DP5YR3&-ds_name=ACS_2009_5YR_G00_&-_lang=en&-_sse=on. No longer accessible.
10. Philip Yancey, *Church, Why Bother? My Personal Pilgrimage,* Growing Deeper series (Grand Rapids, MI: Zondervan, 1998), 32.
11. Alan Hirsch, *The Forgotten Ways: Reactivating the Missional Church* (Grand Rapids, MI: Brazos Press, 2006), 154.

12. Eric Jacobsen, *The Space Between: A Christian Engagement with the Built Environment* (Grand Rapids, MI: Baker Academic, 2012), 194.

13. Alan R. Johnson, *Apostolic Function in 21st Century Missions*, The J. Philip Hogan World Missions Series (Pasadena, CA: William Carey Library, 2009), 152.

14. Mark Batterson, *In the Pit with a Lion on a Snowy Day: How to Survive and Thrive When Opportunity Roars* (New York: MJF Books, 2012), 59.

Chapter 11: The Thing about Money

1. David Olson, "16 Surprising Facts about the American Church, 2006," the American Church Research Project, accessed June 13, 2013, http:// www. theamericanchurch.org, 24.

2. Michael Green, *Evangelism in the Early Church*, rev. ed. (Grand Rapids, MI: Eerdmans, 2004), 300.

Chapter 12: Calling All Church Planters

1. Ed Stetzer, *Planting New Churches in a Postmodern Age* (Nashville, TN: Broadman & Holman, 2003), 10.

2. Warren Bullock (lecture, Northwest University, Kirkland, WA, October 2, 2006).

3. Mark Batterson, *In the Pit with a Lion on a Snowy Day: How to Survive and Thrive When Opportunity Roars* (New York: MJF Books, 2012), 113.

4. Jim Cymbala, "We Got to Change up the Game" (lecture, Orlando Convention Center, Orlando, FL, August 6, 2014).

5. Alan R. Johnson, *Apostolic Function in 21st Century Missions*, J. Philip Hogan World Missions Series (Pasadena, CA: William Carey Library, 2009), 22.

6. Alan Hirsch, *The Forgotten Ways: Reactivating the Missional Church* (Grand Rapids, MI: Brazos Press, 2006), 18.

7. Verlon Fosner, *Dinner Church Handbook: Church Planter's Edition* (Seattle, WA: FindYourFooting, 2014), 9–11.

8. Stetzer, *Planting New Churches in a Postmodern Age*, 185.

9. Hirsch, *The Forgotten Ways,* 18; Michael Green, *Evangelism in the Early Church*, rev. ed. (Grand Rapids: Eerdmans, 2004), 318.

10. Quoted in Rick Rusaw and Eric Swanson, *The Externally Focused Church* (Loveland, CO: Group Publishing Inc., 2004), 29.

Chapter 13: The Family Rescue Business

1. Earl G. Creps, *Off-Road Disciplines: Spiritual Adventures of Missional Leaders*, 1st ed. (San Francisco, CA: Jossey-Bass, 2006), 93.

2. Waldemar Kowalski, "The Book of Romans" (lecture, Northwest University, Kirkland, WA, March 22, 2010).

3. Vinay Samuel, "Mission as Transformation" (lecture to a DMin Class at Oxford Centre for Mission Studies, Oxford, UK, February 23, 2012).

ABOUT THE AUTHOR

Verlon and Melodee Fosner have led a multisite dinner church in Seattle since 1999. In 2014, the Fosners founded the Dinner Church Collective, which is a church-planting network centered on Jesus' dinner church theology. In this decade, when more churches in the United States are declining than thriving, and when eighty churches a week are closing, Verlon and Melodee sensed that a different way of doing church was needed for their ninety-three-year-old Seattle congregation. It soon became obvious that they were not the only ones in need of a different path. There is a lot to be gained when church leaders begin to see open doors in the American landscape that they had previously overlooked. Therein lies the journey for those who will forge a new future for the American church.

The Fosners have three adult children, all of whom are married and bringing on the next generation, which for now means five grandchildren.

For more information go to
CommunityDinners.com
and
DinnerChurchCollective.net